World Trade Order

TRADE 4 PEACE

Dr Abdul Basit Syed

INDIA • SINGAPORE • MALAYSIA

Author Intro

Dr Abdul Basit Syed, FRSA, is a British Indian Peace Activist, Entrepreneur, Writer, and Global influencer campaigning for peace, unity, and equality of access by regularly engaging over 50 countries to create a positive impact worldwide. He is the founder and Chairman of an International NGO, World Humanitarian Drive (WHD), an organisation having Special Consultative Status with the "United Nations Economic and Social Council" (ECOSOC), accredited with Peace, Education, and Trade harmony initiatives globally. He is leading an international campaign for the United Nations to declare Sept 2nd as 'World Moral Day', which marks the ending of World War II. He wrote his thoughts and beliefs about the impacts of morals in a book titled 'Re-engineering Happiness' for adapting morals, which will lead to peace and happiness in the world. This 'World Trade Order' book is envisioned to create a promising reality where conflicts are settled not through hatred and power but through trade exchange, collaboration, and mutual benefits.

Awards and Recognitions:

Fellow of the Royal Society of Arts (FRSA)

Knight of Malta by The Sovereign Order of OSJ, Malta.

Award of Excellence by the United Nations Office On Drugs and Crime (UNODC) & Saudi American Public Relations Affairs Committee (SAPRAC)

International Ambassador honoured by The Mayor of Croydon U.K.

Ambassador for Peace by Universal Peace Federation.

Mahatma Gandhi Award by NRI Welfare Society.

Peace Award by BRICS Alliance.

WORLD HUMANITARIAN DRIVE - UN ECOSOC STATUS

United Nations  Nations Unies

NON-GOVERNMENTAL ORGANIZATIONS BRANCH
OFFICE OF INTERGOVERNMENTAL SUPPORT AND COORDINATION FOR SUSTAINABLE DEVELOPMENT
26th Floor Secretariat Building, United Nations, New York, N.Y. 10017
Telephone: (212) 963-8652; Fax: (212) 963-9248
Website: www.un.org/ecosoc/ngo   Contact: www.un.org/ecosoc/ngo/contact

22 June 2023

Dear NGO Representative,

Subject: Follow-up to the decision of the Economic and Social Council

I am pleased to inform you that on 7 June 2023, the Economic and Social Council (ECOSOC) adopted the recommendation of the Committee on Non-Governmental Organizations (NGOs) to grant special consultative status to your organization, **World Humanitarian Drive**. Please accept our heartfelt congratulations.

Consultative status for an organization enables it to engage in a number of ways with ECOSOC and its subsidiary bodies, the Human Rights Council and, under specific conditions, some meetings of the General Assembly and other intergovernmental bodies, as well as with the United Nations Secretariat. For information on United Nations sessions and events opened to NGOs with consultative status, **please consult our booklet "Working with ECOSOC: an NGO Guide to consultative status"**

(https://www.un.org/sustainabledevelopment)

"The content of this publication has not been approved by the United Nations and does not reflect the views of the United Nations or its officials or Member States".

Contents

Abstract

Envision an optimistic guide where disputes are not resolved with conflicts and hostility but with mutual trade alliances for peaceful co-existence.This vision of "exchange for peace" - the possibility that monetary trade can be encouraged to form connections and cordial relationships between countries (UNCTAD, 2019).

In a world often marked by conflicts and tensions, the role of trade in fostering peace cannot be overstated. The Trade 4 Peace manuscript probes trade's crucial contribution to promoting harmony among nations and highlights the correlation between economic interests and peaceful coexistence (Hoekman and Mavroidis, 2015).

Democratic values are the factors that contribute to the utmost importance in promoting Peace and Harmony between countries.

The nations don't cooperate because of their similar political systems but because of their mutual economic interests. International trade is the critical factor that catalyses this shared prosperity (Crespo and Simoes, 2021). When nations are engaged in trade and business, they will also be in peaceful relations.

Trade agreements and partnerships provide a platform for resolving disputes and conflicts peacefully. By establishing rules and mechanisms for addressing trade-related grievances, countries can navigate disputes through dialogue and negotiation, averting potential escalations into violence (Lim, Deborah Kay Elms and Low, 2012). Trade is a diplomatic engagement and conflict resolution channel, promoting stability and peace (Lucie Qian Xia, 2024).

'The global trade interdependence promotes and supports peaceful coexistence between nations'.

01

The Significance of Trade in Promoting Peace

Economic interdependence through trade plays a pivotal role in reducing the likelihood of conflicts between nations. When countries engage in trade, they become mutually reliant on each other for goods and services, creating a vested interest in maintaining peaceful relations (Gitman, Mcdaniel and Shah, 2023). This interdependence fosters a sense of shared prosperity and cooperation, serving as a powerful deterrent to conflict escalation (Narang, Gartzke and Kroenig, 2015).

When two countries are distressed about trespassing or hostile aggression, expanding arms and ammunition in the territories and allied nations is inevitable (Grehan, 2013). War is one kind of manifestation, but the objective of the combatant countries was to defend the military interests of their country and its allies. The aggressiveness in the expansion of the military, border infiltration and encroachment are a few examples of armed Peace. The uncompromising engagement between the countries costs much military expenditure, negatively impacting the state's growth and development (Prabhakaran Paleri, 2022). Even if the countries have similar democratic values or cultures, when they still lack economic ties, Peace between them is not probable (Arie Marcelo Kacowicz, 2000).

Bilateral or multilateral trade is the most significant factor in reducing conflict between nations. A regional trade agreement between the countries will lead to close integration ties toward Peace and security (Buckley, Vai Io Lo, and Boulle, 2008). Economic interdependence and bilateral trade are the most significant factors contributing to the countries' peaceful relations (Dunning, Mikoto Usui, and International Economic Association. World Congress, 1987).

According to the World Trade Organization, countries more open to international trade tend to experience higher economic growth than those with more restrictive trade policies (Aaditya Mattoo, Stern and Gianni Zanini, 2008).

Organisations like the World Trade Organization (WTO) serve as forums for countries to address trade disputes through legal mechanisms, ensuring a rules-based system that fosters peaceful conflict resolution (Fouad Sabry, 2023).

(I)   Building Extensions

Trade has forever been demonstrated as an astonishing resource for settling inconsistencies. The following are a couple of focal issues to consider.

a) Economic growth

One key benefit of international trade for countries is the potential for economic growth. s. This mutual trade, in turn, can lead to increased investment, job creation, and overall economic development (Durlauf and Blume, 2010).

b) Diversification of industries

Participating in international trade allows countries to diversify their industries and reduce reliance on a single sector. It will help mitigate the risks associated with economic downturns in specific industries and promote overall stability in the country (Sami Mahroum and Yasser Al-Saleh, 2016).

Countries like Singapore and South Korea have successfully diversified their economies through international trade, focusing on high-tech industries and services to drive growth (Papageorgiou and Mr Nicola Spatafora, 2012).

c) Access to resources

International trade enables countries to access resources and inputs that may not be readily available domestically, which leads to cost savings, increased efficiency, and improved competitiveness in various industries (Smith, 2013).

Japan, a country with limited natural resources, relies heavily on imports to meet its energy and raw material needs. These imports allow it to sustain its manufacturing sector and remain competitive globally (Adams, 2010).

d) Advancement of technology

Engaging in trade with technologically advanced countries can spur innovation and technological advancement in domestic industries. By adopting and adapting foreign technologies, countries can enhance productivity, improve product quality, and stay competitive in the global marketplace (Preker et al., 2010).

Silicon Valley in the United States has long been a hub for technological innovation, attracting talent and investment worldwide and driving industry advancements (Schilling, 2023).

e) Monetary dependence

Trade creates financial dependence and recognises the distinctive benefits of maintaining good relations with other countries. When nations rely upon other countries for resources, tourism, employment, military protection or political trade, they are more reluctant to engage in activities which could hinder the trade movement (Yannick Malevergne and Didier Sornette, 2006).

f) Social exchange

In addition to economic benefits, international trade fosters cultural exchange and understanding between nations. Through the exchange of goods, services, and ideas, countries can build relationships, promote mutual respect, and celebrate diversity (Engelbrecht, 2015).

(II) Trade – An Ancient Way to Concordance

For centuries, during ancient and medieval times, economic benefits were the primary reason for conquering other countries.

What factors contribute to promoting harmony between the countries? Is it the economic interest or political democracy? History shows that nations interdependent on trade do not wage war quickly and remain peaceful as they share common interests. Any mild dispute would be resolved without using force to retain violence, as both countries would be at a loss (Daily, 2019).

The Silk Road, an ancient network of trade routes connecting Asia with Europe, facilitated commercial transactions and enabled the exchange of ideas, technologies, and cultural practices. These trade routes played a pivotal role in contributing to cross-cultural understanding and harmony between East and West (Captivating History, 2020).

After World War II, there was significant peace worldwide, and occasional conflicts were observed between a few countries. Political analysts have related liberal conduct, democratic forms of government, and interdependent trade among the states as the critical reasons for this stable harmony. Nations adopted policies that emphasised the most benefit of acquiring profits, and free trade contributed the most. Due to trade, even countries commanding minor military capacity flourished and prospered with Peace (Chitadze, 2022).

We must investigate some current genuine models where trade exchange plays a crucial role in propelling concordance.

The improvement of the European Union, which was initially formed as an economic bloc, is an incredible portrayal of how shared exchange can catalyse harmony and unity. By empowering monetary support and fusing among European nations, the EU has hindered inconsistencies by strengthening economic ties among member states and promoting collaboration through trade agreements (Erik Oddvar Eriksen and John Erik Fossum, 2015).

China and Taiwan have maintained economic ties through trade exchange despite their political differentiations. This financial relationship has thwarted outrageous military confrontations and reliability. Despite their geopolitical differences, China and the United States have maintained a complex economic relationship driven by trade, highlighting how economic interdependence can act as a stabilising force (Robert Paul Weller, 2019).

Countries with affluence could exploit trade associations for their benefit by provoking dependence and misuse. Ensuring fair and unbiased financial partnerships is crucial for building long-lasting goodwill (Mohamad Riad El Ghonemy, 1998).

Trade facilitates cultural exchange by converging people from different backgrounds and promoting mutual understanding and perception. By engaging in trade, nations are exposed to their trading partners' customs and values, fostering respect and tolerance for diversity. This cultural exchange is essential for building peaceful relations based on mutual shared values (Heritage and Strozenberg, 2019).

"Trade has the power to unite nations through shared prosperity and mutual respect, paving the way for a more peaceful world."

02

Trade 4 Peace - Accreditation

Trade 4 Peace is constructed to improve the working conditions of organisations by ensuring fair and ethical practices. Trade 4 Peace accreditation is a system that guarantees ethical and fair practices to benefit workers and communities worldwide (Steger, 2010).

An organisation will satisfy social and environmental standards by fulfilling the employment requirements under the categories mentioned below.

- Gender Equality
- Differently-abled
- Abolition of Child Labour
- Diversity, Equity&Inclusion
- Basic Human Rights
- Environmental Responsibility

(I) Impact & Scope

a) Social, Economy & Environment

Trade 4 Peace accreditation ensures that workers are equally paid, work in safe conditions, and are socially responsible. One of the most significant benefits of this accreditation is the workers' economic empowerment. By receiving this accreditation, organisations can increase productivity, thereby improving the livelihood of the workers (Nedumpara, Satwik Shekhar and Venkataraman, 2021).

This accreditation also promotes social and sustainable environmental practices, which help protect nature and ensure the industry's longevity.

b) Community Welfare

Trade 4 Peace accreditation will positively impact the communities as a whole. By supporting this accreditation, consumers are helping to build a stronger community by promoting social justice, fair labour practices and sustainable development. It also helps to empower women, an opportunity for differently-abled, and equality for all marginalised groups by giving them a voice in the decision-making process and providing them with opportunities for economic independence (Sami Mahroum and Yasser Al-Saleh, 2016).

c) Prospect of the Accreditation

By choosing the accreditation, consumers can help support social, economic & environmental causes and positively impact workers' lives worldwide. As the demand for fair and ethical products sourced and manufactured rises globally, Trade 4 Peace accreditation is likely to play an increasingly important role in the global economy. By supporting the accreditation initiative, consumers can help ensure a sustainable future for all (Breitenberg, 1993).

Trade 4 Peace accreditation is a powerful tool for promoting social justice, economic empowerment and sustainable environmental responsibility. This accreditation is not a mere trademark – it is a constructive movement to change the way for trade and globalisation. By supporting the accreditation, we can make a significant difference in the lives of others (Adams, 2010).

(II)   Basis for Standard Operating Procedures – SOP

Trade 4 Peace is envisioned with initiatives to promote a functional and positive working atmosphere. The basic SOPs incorporate the requirements to create a positive and practical framework for an ethical working environment (Cox et al., 2014).

Despite their scale, implementing Standard Operating Procedure (SOP) in every working environment ensures efficiency, consistency, and productivity. SOPs are methodical instructions that outline the specific tasks or procedures to be carried out in an organisation. We will establish the importance of SOPs in the work environment and their contribution to overall productivity and quality (Haar, 2008).

(III)   Benefits of Implementing SOPs

a) Consistency & Quality Assurance

SOPs help maintain operations consistency by ensuring that every procedure is performed uniformly. This consistency improves quality assurance as employees follow standardised procedures, resulting in fewer errors and a high-quality output (Gipps, 1994).

b) Training & Onboarding

The SOPs provide a valuable training tool, especially for new employees. By delivering standardised documented instructions on performed tasks, SOPs can help streamline the onboarding process and minimise the duration of training (Davila and Pina-Ramirez, 2018).

c) Risk Management and Compliance

By documenting best practices and safety protocols, SOPs help mitigate potential risks and ensure that employees adhere to industry regulations and standards. This proactive approach promotes a safe work environment and minimises legal liabilities (Steinberg, 2011).

d) Process Optimisation and Efficiency

SOPs help identify bottlenecks, inefficiencies, redundancies, and areas for improvement. This structured approach enables companies to optimise operations, enhance productivity, and reduce wastage (Xin, 2013).

Brands, retailers, and manufacturers should take responsibility for the working conditions and environment for the workers with fair and ethical standards. The following protocols are the basic principles and rights at work to achieve ethical trading based on recommendations and derivation from the International Labour Organization (ILO) (International Labour Office, 2004).

We need coordinated policies to facilitate education, technical training, and innovation. By having a contextual analysis and supporting standards, we will achieve exponential changes and growth in the business.

In conclusion, SOPs ensure workplace efficiency, consistency, and productivity. By implementing SOPs, organisations can benefit from improved quality assurance, streamlined training processes, risk management, process optimisation, and progressive accountability. Investing time and resources in developing and maintaining SOPs can lead to significant long-term benefits for businesses of all sizes. Embracing SOPs as integral components of operations can pave the way for sustainable growth and success in today's competitive business structure (Fleisher and Bensoussan, 2022).

03

Gender Equality

In today's modern world, the drive for gender equality in the workplace has never been stronger. As we strive towards a more inclusive and diverse environment, it is significant to address the challenges women face in various industries. The existing gender imbalances at the macro and micro levels significantly impact society (Ridgeway, 2011).

The World Economic Forum (WEF) 2006 introduced the 'Global Gender Gap Index' based on economic opportunities, education, health, and political leadership. The Global Gender Gap 2023 report includes 146 countries with 14 indicators as validation data. The top 9 countries, Iceland, Norway, Finland, New Zealand, Sweden, Germany, Nicaragua, Namibia, and Lithuania, have closed nearly 80% of the gender gap (Ng et al., 2021).

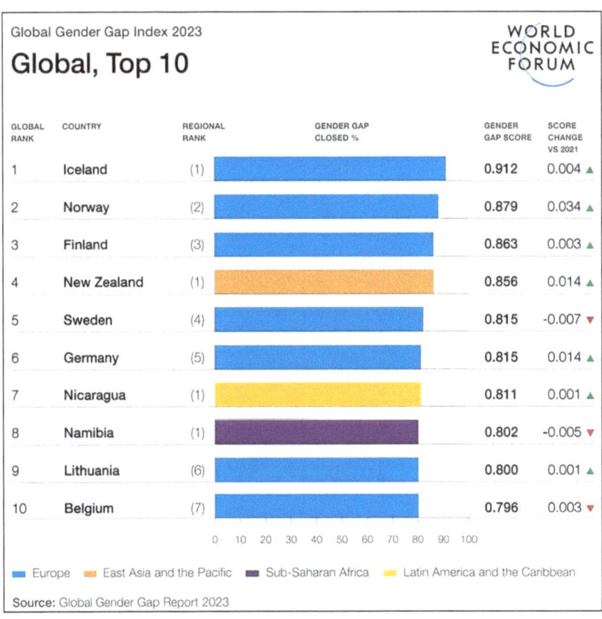

The latest data from the International Labour Organization (ILO) shows that the global unemployment rate is approximately 4.3% for men and 4.5% for women.

(I) Significance of Gender Equality

We must address gender equality for fairness, justice, and basic human rights. It is essential to create an equally balanced, thriving workforce with equal opportunities to succeed. Here are some main reasons why gender equality matters significantly.

a) Promoting Diversity & Innovation

A diverse working environment leads to increased creativity, innovation, and productivity. When men and women are given equal opportunities, companies benefit from a broader talent pool of various perspectives and ideas, which can promote growth and success.

b) Ensuring Economic Empowerment

It is essential to close the gender wage gap and guarantee that women have equal access to career advancement opportunities and gender equality in the workplace. When women are empowered with economic authority, the workplace and society gain from economic growth.

(II) Challenges in the Workforce

Despite the progressive results in recent years, women still face significant challenges in the workplace that hinder their success and advancement. Some of the common barriers include:

a) Bias & Stereotypes

Women often face biased opinions and stereotyping in the work environment, which can impact their career progression and opportunities. Addressing these constant biases is pivotal in creating a more inclusive and supportive environment for all employees.

b) Lack of Leadership

Even though many organisations employ women as per the norms, the critical challenge women face is the lack of representation in leadership roles. Gender diversity at the top levels of organisations is essential for assembling propositions and promoting a gender-equal work culture.

c) Covid Pandemic

Gender Equality and women's rights are essential to getting through this pandemic together, to recovering faster and to building a better future for everyone," said U.N. Secretary-General Antonio Guterres.

The Ambassadors of 124 UN Member States and Observers committed to preventing and addressing gender-based violence as pivotal agendas in their national proposals.

Almost 70% of frontline health workers have participated significantly as nurses, caretakers, midwives, and community health workers during this pandemic. Despite the crucial contribution made by women in the global pandemic caused by women, and despite the factor, they are underpaid and possess fewer leadership positions in healthcare.

The U.N. Women's Regional Office of Asia and Pacific (ROAP) survey shows the gendered effects of the COVID pandemic in Asia and the Pacific. The analysis from 8 out of 11 Asian Pacific countries states that fewer women receive essential information about COVID-19 due to less access to mobile phones, the internet, and academic knowledge.

According to the survey, more than half of the women cannot seek medical attention or visit the doctor and have difficulty acquiring hygiene and healthcare products. Most women are employed in an informal workforce with inaccessible health care and without insurance covered by employers, making them vulnerable to diseases.

As trade and businesses shut down, it creates disproportionate devastation for women working in the informal economy, drifting into poverty. We can build a better societal future by including them in all responses and recovery decisions.

The restriction in movements and lockdowns damages women suffering from gender-based and domestic violence as they are confined at home with limited social support services during COVID-19. Women play a significant role in nurturing the health and safety routines in the household. It is imperative to assist with adequate information and support them in encouraging the practices to combat COVID-19.

(III)   Proposed Strategies for Change:

To promote gender equality in the workplace, organisations must address the fundamental causes of inequality by implementing strategic initiatives and policies. Below are some effective strategies for promoting gender equality:

a) Equal Pay and Benefits

Regardless of gender, ensuring equal pay and benefits for all employees is the first positive step towards gender equality. Companies should conduct regular pay audits to identify and address any discrepancies in pay compensation. The persistent disparities in wages for women are drastically low compared to men, which means women are working more and earning less in bold comparison.

b) Gender-equal Pay Gap

We need to analyse the inequality of gender pay in the job market to address the increasing number of women in the informal job industry falling into impoverishment. It creates a domino effect on life savings and pensions for retirement. Nearly 40 % of women do not subscribe to pensions, health insurance, and social benefits due to the high margin of pay differences. We cannot meet the Sustainable Development Goals targets aimed at ending poverty and gender equality at this current pay gap rate.

The average earnings of full-time working women are around 80% compared to men's earnings with similar positions and environments. This gender wage gap is worse in women of colour, who experience racial and ethnic discrimination and face wider gaps in wages. The Census Bureau income data, 2017 shows that a woman of colour has to work until 86 years old to equal the men's earnings till 60 years old.

Women are persisting with inequality and grappling with long-standing biases ingrained in workplace culture. The practices and attitudes of workplace gender partiality that demote morally and limit their career advancement remain unchallenged.

c) Bridge the gap

Centralised minimum living wages will favour low-paid workers, benefiting women exponentially. When basic income increases, women can avail of national policies and benefits such as social protection, paid maternity leave, health and hazardous insurance, and child care support. It is imperative to include informal workers who are predominantly women to profit under social reforms.

Enrolling in a collective union or organisation and having the freedom to voice their issues plays a crucial role. In the United Kingdom, non-unionised women receive 30% less than women enrolled in unions.

Regular check-ups and internal equity audits ensure equal gender pay, and if discrepancies occur, management should resolve them by implementing correct practices.

Recruitment and promotion should be compared equally with men and women with similar skills and experiences without bias for recruitment, advertising, and wages. Fixing salary ranges for a particular job and being transparent in data are significant in closing the gender pay gap in organisations.

How do we bridge the gap?

1. Proposing a joint meeting with employers and unions to address the pay gap.
2. Making comparisons with data and guidance to identify the causes.
3. Urge the employer to take action for an equal pay audit.
4. Analysing the basic policies of recruitment and training.
5. Promoting equal shared parental leave among men and reassuring phased comeback from maternity leave.

(IV)   Launching Campaigns

Do you know that there is a 23% global gender pay gap? Globally, women are making 23% less than men; at this rate, it will take 70 years to bridge the gender pay gap. There will be no equal pay until 2069.

The global region-wise gender gap report by the World Economic Forum (WEF) shows an alarming gap of nearly 50 to 200 years of equal pay as men.

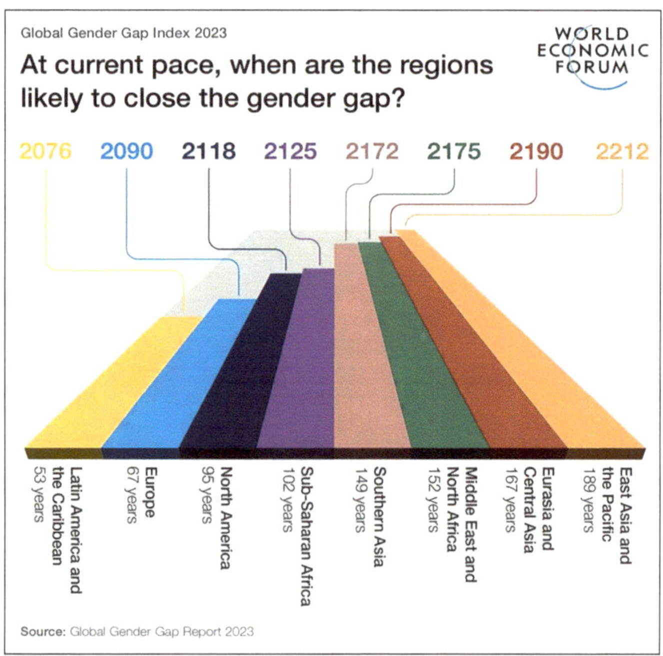

a) Stop the robbery – United Nations Women

The initiative launched by United Nations Women as #stoptherobbery – Equal Pay Campaign is to create public awareness for equal pay for work of equal value. This social experiment campaign aimed to create a long-lasting impact on gender pay differences and change perceptions. The campaign showed the pay differences between men and women for the same services rendered.

By elevating and addressing the 'Armchair Activism' concerning the pay gap framed as the biggest robbery in the #stoptherobbery campaign, it is to gain the world's attention to close the gender pay gap.

The director of the Equality Department of the International Trade Union Confederation (ITUC), Chidi King, states that setting minimum living wages is the quickest way to speed up the process. Women are majorly present in informal and depleted wages.

The inequality between the genders in society and the workplace portrays men's roles as primary decision-makers and women's roles as caregivers, displaying the work's indifferences as undermined and devalued. A job in male-dominated work sectors such as mining or construction is the same or similar to a job in female-dominated sectors such as caregiver sectors but invariably paid less. The indifferent perception of valuing similar jobs has to evolve, as acknowledged by the International Labour Organization (ILO) Equal Remuneration Convention, 1951 (No.100).

b) Bridge that Gap – UNISON

UNISON, the public service union representing most women in the U.K., led a nationwide campaign to equal the workplace pay gap. According to the Office for National Statistics 2017, data shows that men earn 18% more than women for the same work. In the U.K., organisations must declare the gender pay data if they have more than 250 employees.

"Proper enforceable sanctions and clear end date will force reluctant bosses to be transparent and stop the disparity. Women have failed in the workplace for too long, so these commitments are long overdue," quoted UNISON general secretary Dave Prentis, commenting on Labour's plans to eliminate the gender pay gap by 2030.

Angie Roberts from the National Executive Council (NEC) said, "We call on all the employers to take urgent action, and the fight for equality is far from over, and it is getting wider."

How do these campaigns create a ripple, and whether they make any outcome?

The Glasgow Council has agreed to compensate 548 million pounds for women in catering, cleaning, and caring departments. This deal depicts the loss of pay due to the grading system since 2007. This pay settlement exemplifies recognising equal value and addressing the dispute.

These campaigns create visibility and awareness to create a solid position to negotiate upgraded policies and practices to mend the gender pay gap.

(V)   Implementation

a) Mentorship and Sponsorship Programmes

Upskilling and career-developing programmes can help women navigate challenges and advance in their careers. Companies can provide valuable support and guidance by pairing women employees with experienced mentors, which will benefit the company in the long run.

b) Flexible Work Policies

Flexible Work Arrangements (FWA's) are work structures that provide flexibility regarding work schedule, location, and hours worked in which work is completed. Flexible arrival or departure timings, compressed work across the week, and sharing jobs will empower the arrangements to comply appropriately.

Implementing flexible work policies, such as remote work options and flexible hours, can help women balance their professional and personal responsibilities. After the Covid pandemic, many organisations switched to remote work, and because of this, women could continue without compromising their careers. This flexibility is essential for promoting diversity and inclusion in the workplace.

Over ten years, 131 countries introduced 274 legal and regulatory forms supporting gender equality in their structures. There have been progressive changes; we can see an increased number of girls accessing education and a decline in maternal mortality by 38% between 2000 and 2017. (Beijing platform of action)

The U.S. Bureau of Labour Statistics shows that 4.1 million employed women manage multiple jobs. More than 64% are primary or co-income earners in their families, which is vital for economic growth.

The reality of women's rights challenges remains understated, as it is in the workplace, politics, and leadership.

Women's work is undervalued mainly in the informal workforce, such as domestic workers, and legal unions and policies do not support part-time workers and farm labourers. Women are preferably employed and continuously underpaid as child care providers, care workers, receptionists, housekeepers, and teaching professionals, rather than their male coworkers. These adverse effects lead to less access to education, talent improvement, and health detriment.

c) Improved Working Conditions

Women encounter various workplace issues and challenges and many societal factors. Even though women do favourable things to improve their careers, access is often denied to senior job positions or waived, as those are vital for uplifting morally and career-wise. Organisations invest hugely in sourcing, developing, and retaining talents, and it is crucial to balance gender equality in the workforce to minimise job attrition.

Technology enables us to work in a coffee shop just as in-office cubicles. This pandemic transformed us to use alternative ways to think and analyse solutions because of lockdown norms and work-from-home.

Gender discrimination and offensive sexual advancement are defined by the Equal Employment Opportunity Commission (EOCC) "as unwelcome advances, requests for sexual favours and other verbal or physical conduct of a sexual nature…[that]explicitly or implicitly affects an individual's employment, unreasonably interferes with an individual's work performance, or creates an intimidating, hostile, or offensive work environment.

The survey of Work in Freedom by ILO states that nearly 20% of women suffered sexual harassment in Hong Kong, Italy it is 55.4%, European Union reports 40-50%. These numbers are officially reported grievances, but the unreported cases are twice the numbers. Research shows that young, financially independent women, single or divorced, and migrant status are majorly vulnerable to abuse.

The victims undergo psychological detriment, reduced self-esteem, substance abuse, leaving employment, and, in the worst cases, they commit suicide. The claims reduce productivity due to absenteeism, demotivating team spirit, and hindering progress. The sexual harassment claims will lead to a morally declined perception of the organisation by the public. Taking timely, informative actions to consider the victim and create awareness will reduce the adverse conception. Educating and creating awareness about sexism in the workplace and, if needed, using expertise to develop awareness about bias and sexism.

Many countries have incorporated legal frameworks to enforce the paramount importance of combating sexual harassment in the workplace.

Criminal Laws	India, Tanzania
Labour Codes	Chile, Thailand
Laws targeting sexual harassment	Brazil, Belize, Philipines, Israel
National Human Rights Legislation	Canada, Fiji, Newzealand
Laws on safe working conditions	Netherlands

Even if the legislation and guidelines are in place as checkpoints for prevention and redress grievances, we are responsible for educating, creating awareness, and acting sensibly.

d) Affecting Social Reforms

According to the Women at Work Trends 2016 report by the International Labour Organization (ILO), over 65% of women of retirement age are without a pension, which means 200 million women are denied any social protection compared to 115 million men. Nearly all countries have subsidised schemes and policies supporting maternity during employment, but 60 % of women workers (750 million) do not benefit from maternity leave rights.

Awareness of statutory rights and policies, implementation in the workplace, discrimination, and social extradition are the leading causes of the non-availing of national social protection. The United Nations' Sustainable Development Goals (SDGs), which aim to eradicate poverty and improve social upliftment targets, are hindered by the Gender pay gap. Reducing the gap will strengthen and boost the SDGs and enhance social upliftment.

Giving a chance to all genders is economically significant as it benefits society. Eliminating gender disparity at all levels in jobs and wages will positively impact economic growth. Incorporating gender perspective in trade policy and implementation will reduce the widening gap in job placements.

In conclusion, gender equality in the workplace is crucial to creating a fair and inclusive environment where all genders can thrive equally. Closing the widening gender gap should be a priority for all legislators, policymakers, and organisations to recover from poverty and strengthen economic growth.

Organisations can promote diversity and equality by addressing the challenges faced by women and implementing effective strategies for positive change. It is time to break down the barriers and build a more inclusive future for all employees.

Remember, the journey towards gender equality is an ongoing process. It requires collective effort and commitment from everyone. Let's work together to create a workplace where everyone has an equal opportunity to succeed.

Trade 4 Peace is compiled with fairness and equality, aligning with the UN Sustainable Development Goals (SDGs).

(IV) SDG – Targets & Indicators	
5 GENDER EQUALITY	
Target 5.1	End all forms of discrimination against all women and girls everywhere
Indicators 5.1.1	Whether or not legal frameworks are in place to promote, enforce, and monitor equality and non-discrimination on the basis of sex
Target 5.4	Recognize and value unpaid care and domestic care work through the provision of public services, infrastructure and social protection policies and the promotion of shared responsibility within the household and the family as nationally appropriate
Indicators 5.4.1	Proportion of time spent on unpaid domestic and care work, by sex, age and location
Target 5.5	Ensure women's full and effective participation and equal opportunities for leadership at all levels of decision-making in political, economic and public life
Indicators 5.5.2	Proportion of women in managerial positions
Target 5.C	Adopt and strengthen sound policies and enforceable legislation for the promotion of gender equality and the empowerment of all women and girls

4 QUALITY EDUCATION	
Target 4.4	By 2030, substantially increase the number of youth and adults who have relevant skills, including technical and vocational skills, for employment, decent jobs and entrepreneurship
Indicators 4.4.1	Proportion of youth and adults with information and communications technology (ICT) skills, by type of skill
10 REDUCED INEQUALITIES	
Target 10.2	By 2030, empower and promote the social, economic and political inclusion of all, irrespective of age, sex, disability, race, ethnicity, origin, religion or economic or other status
Indicators 10.2.1	Proportion of people living below 50 per cent of median income, by age, and persons with disabilities

04

Employment of Differently-abled

In today's world, we cannot underrate the importance of inclusivity, and one crucial aspect is addressing different-abled challenges in the workplace. We must explore the key issues that different-abled individuals face in work environments and provide functional insights into creating a more inclusive atmosphere.

Differently-abled is a diverse phenomenon that impacts individuals in various ways. It is crucial to address the challenges faced by people with disabilities and work towards implementing practical solutions to create a more inclusive society.

Differently-abled can be physical, cognitive, sensory, or mental health-related issues. Each type of disability presents unique challenges and requires customary support to ensure equal opportunities for all individuals.

(I)   Challenges by Differently -abled

- Social Stigma
- Accessibility Issues
- Employment Barriers

a) Understanding Differently-abled in the Workplace

Differently -abled people cover a broad spectrum of conditions that may impact an individual's physical, cognitive, or emotional abilities. These challenges are apparent in the workplace, including accessibility barriers, preconceived notions, and unconscious social stigma.

Differently-abled is no inability; our Trade 4 Peace policies aim to integrate differently-abled individuals by acknowledging and incorporating them into the workforce by enhancing employment opportunities. We can see positive societal changes if we increase awareness even at the micro-level. Our proactive initiation will ensure the incorporation of differently-abled individuals into all government and private-sector employment schemes. People with special needs can perform all jobs by providing the right environment and conditions. Several studies across all countries reveal significantly lower employment in differently-abled sectors, which leads to poverty.

The United Nations Convention on the Rights of Persons with Disabilities (CRPD) under Article27 - states, "Recognises the right of persons with disabilities to work, on an equal basis with others, this includes the opportunity to gain a living by work freely chosen or accepted in a labour market and work environment that is open, inclusive and accessible to persons with disabilities." It also prohibits all forms of discrimination and prejudice. It promotes training, among other benefits, to encourage the employment of differently-abled as any form of disability should not be considered a hindrance to achieving their goals.

The concept of disability is used in the Vocational Rehabilitation and Employment (Disabled Persons) Convention, 1983 (No 159) (ILO 1983). Article 1.1 states, "The disabled means an individual whose prospects of securing, retaining and advancing in suitable employment are substantially reduced due to a duty recognised physical or mental impairment."

The World Economic Forum (WEF) statistics of European labour market data show that the percentage of persons with disabilities in the labour market is lower than individuals without disabilities by 60% vs 82%.

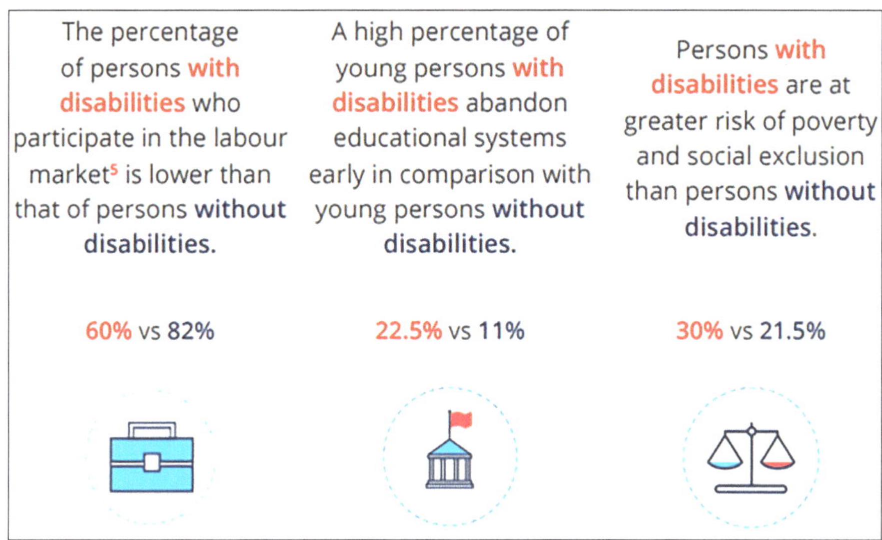

The World Report on Disability by the World Health Organization and The World Bank data shows that more than one billion people in the world live with some form of disability worldwide.

The primary goal is to strive for the right to equal opportunity and treatment of disabled persons. The objective is to create the same employment with income-generating as others.

The International Labour Organization (ILO) has derived three measures to attain this.

1. To empower the disabled individual with technical assistance and training required to cope with the job definition.
2. To familiarise the surroundings in the workplace in terms of jobs, machinery tools and promotional support to overcome discrimination.
3. To ensure the fulfilment of quota allocation or sanction levy under schemes.

According to the United Nations Development Programme (UNDP), the primary goal of UN Sustainable Development Goal 17 is to

"Significantly increase the availability of high-quality, timely, and reliable data disaggregated by disability – Target 17.18."

We have roughly about 10% of the population worldwide, and 150 million children are differently-abled. The statistics show that the chances of getting employment are above 50%, that everyone doesn't register as a differently-abled person, and that there is a lack of verified data from many countries.

The World Report on Disability by the World Health Organization (WHO) states that the employment rate difference between disabled individuals in the overall population varies from 30% to 92%.

Individuals	Percent					
	Low-income countries		High-income countries		All countries	
	Not disabled	Disabled	Not disabled	Disabled	Not disabled	Disabled
Male	71.2	58.6*	53.7	36.4*	64.9	52.8*
Female	31.5	20.1*	28.4	19.6*	29.9	19.6*
18–49	58.8	42.9*	54.7	35.2*	57.6	41.2*
50–59	62.9	43.5*	57.0	32.7*	60.9	40.2*
60 and over	38.1	15.1*	11.2	3.9*	26.8	10.4*

Note: Estimates are weighted using WHS post-stratified weights, when available (probability weights otherwise), and age-standardized. * *t*-test suggests significant difference from "Not disabled" at 5%.
Source (43).

Studies show a steady rise in the numbers. The factors causing these are armed violence and conflicts, which result in injury, malnutrition among children, diseases and substance abuse.

(II)   Disability Discrimination

Discriminating on the grounds of physical or mental disability and being treated with less advantage than others without a disability should be forbidden. In simple terms, there is less ability with restriction to perform a variety of activities. It isn't easy to define that a person with a disability is not fully functional compared to others. How to categorise a visually impaired person who sings better than others? How do you classify a hard-of-hearing person who is well-versed in the IT industry? Disabled persons still do daily chores, work and run a family. The restrictions in a few areas have created a stigma in our society.

We have famous icons who have inspired millions and have contributed more than others in all areas of specialisation, such as Ludwig Van Beethoven, Frida Kahlo, Franklin D. Roosevelt, Stephen Hawking, Helen Keller, John Nash, and more. The world is inspired and has gained its spirits of wisdom and knowledge.

(III)   Difficulties and Barriers to Employment

Improvements in environmental conditions and facilities will reduce dependency and restrictions on the workforce and society. Even with the facilities, there would be barriers to a certain degree, but we could achieve full integration in the workplace with the right opportunity and support optimisation.

The Vocational Rehabilitation and Employment [Disabled persons] Convention 1983 9(No 159) and United Nations Standard Rules on the Equalisation of Opportunities for Persons with Disabilities (UN 1993) have newfound policies and programmes to facilitate the upliftment of people with disabilities.

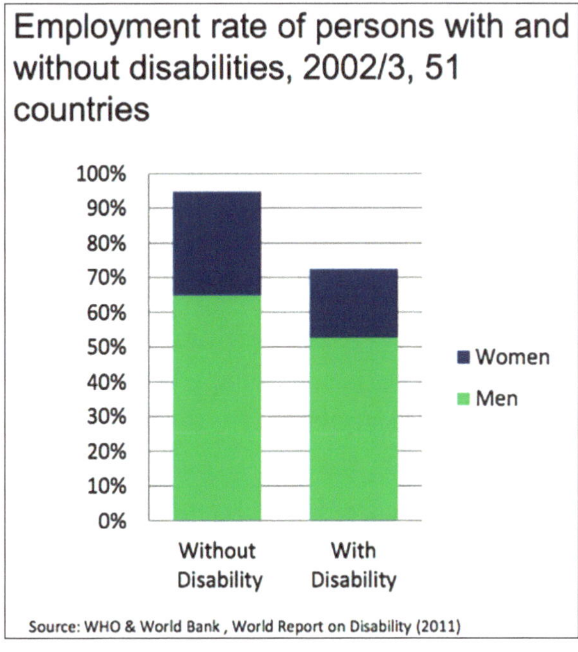

(IV) Quota Schemes

The UN Convention on the Rights of Persons with Disabilities expands from 7 to 21 differently-abled conditions and focuses on a new process for procuring disability certification for institutions.

According to International Labour Organization – Promoting Employment Opportunities for People with Disabilities: Quota Schemes (Vol.1)

The employment quotas allocate employees with disabilities in public and private sectors. Over 100 countries have had quotas in national legislation for decades, and many countries have followed suit. In the past, there were negative views about the working capacity of differently-abled individuals; recently, it has emerged as favourable to anti-discrimination legislation. There are measures to compensate employers who fulfil the quota and sanction those who do not adhere to the allocations.

ILO Convention on Vocation of Rehabilitation and Employment of Disabled Persons (C.No.159) of 1983, remodelled version consists of 2 volumes: introducing or making recommendations for new systems or revising existing ones. The second one is to provide quota schemes combined with anti-discrimination legislation worldwide.

Over 52 countries have quota and non-discrimination laws varying from 1% to 10% in public and private sectors—a lot of crucial provisions implemented to ensure the smooth application of the quotas.

Only people with permanent or long-term physical, intellectual and sensory impairments are qualified and registered as disabled to obtain the quota by assessments. There is an additional provision for 'Women with disabilities'; only Albania and South Korea have implemented this quota system. In Albania, differently-abled women are motivated to apply for employment aided with mandatory insurance paid by the government on behalf of the employer. In South Korea, the government financially assists owners who employ women rather than differently-abled men.

The benefits and concessions of the employer who employs people with disabilities are entitled to avail of wage subsidies, financial incentives, tax exemptions, subsidies for up-gradation and reduction or exemption from social security contributions. In a few countries, additional points are given to companies which prefer to hire persons with a disability while bidding for government contracts.

In non-compliance with quota obligation, employers have imposed a levy or fine designated to a fund or state budget—most funds are affiliated with vocational training and rehabilitation programmes for differently-abled persons.

Few countries have adopted other ways to support the quota obligations, such as offering preferential subcontract options and purchasing products or services from employers who hire people with differently abled qualities. The Labour and Employment Promotion Ministry oversees enforcing and complying with quotas in the private sector. The National Council checks the public sector for the Integration of Persons with Disabilities [CONADIS].

a) Facts and Reality

The United Nations Department of Economic and Social Affairs Disability states,

Fact 1: It is challenging to extract the exact data on employment of disability, and 80% to 90% of working-age with disability are unemployed in developing countries. This number is twice that of non-disability persons.

Fact 2: Disabled persons are not perceived as the potential workforce as understanding and acceptance are hard to come by as discrimination and false beliefs about being unable to work equally as others.

Fact 3: Hiring persons with disabilities will incorporate them in social inclusion with diverse workgroups. Adaptation results in better solutions and builds social reputation.

(V)   Implementing and Aiding Adaptation

Including differently-abled people in the workforce is more critical than ever; filling quota schemes, compliance, extending support, and corporate social responsibility will not be sufficient. Employers should be given various tax benefits and amenities if they have persons with special needs in their workforce. The Disability Equality Index (DEI) is the benchmark tool to assess Fortune 1000 against disability inclusion in the workplace. The recent Accenture report found that companies that include differently-abled persons have achieved 28% higher revenue, 30% profit margin and twice the net income than other industrial competitors.

David Casey, VP of Workforce Strategies & Chief Diversity Officer at CVS Health, stated, "People with disabilities tend to be some of the most creative, innovative and, quite frankly, most loyal employees. A person with disability wakes up every day thinking about innovation – that is skillset."

a) Creating Awareness

Training Human Resource professionals and managers to broaden their knowledge and understanding of different talents by hiring and improving progress is essential. While only a few organisations guide businesses to assist on resource networks on special needs person inclusion, many are unaware of tapping the full potential. Education, accessibility to the working environment, and awareness in the workplace are crucial for the successful deployment of the initiation. The management should establish different evaluation processes, assessments, and guidelines for smooth incorporation.

b) Soft Skills & Technical Training:

"It is especially critical to provide the training to individuals with disabilities, so they understand all aspects of how to be successful at work," said John D Kemp, President and CEO of Viscardi Center - Nonprofit for Disabled Adults & Children. Developing on-the-job training must be in tailored content for each or similar groups or as individual needs. The employer should provide training and coaching for communication, organisational skillset, workplace ethics, and techniques, as it is equally essential for a person with special needs to blend in with society.

c) Linking of Volunteer Support Groups

The support group provides a common medium for them to connect and receive guidance and moral support. It is an imperative and highly essential measure to boost morale, as working with non-disabled workers can be challenging at times. Sharing ideas, inputs, and support from volunteer groups, such as inclusion in Employee Resource Groups (ERGs), will drastically improve professional relationships.

d) Flexible Employment Contracts:

Flexible and part-time working policy, Flexi-time employment contract can be applied if necessary. Asking for flexible working hours may be suited within reasonable adjustment, but lower working hours result in less financial benefit. Remote and alternative schedules can provide opportunities and create revenue that will be of mutual benefit.

e) Improved Working Conditions:

We can harness smooth work-life transactions by providing good infrastructure and effectively implementing modifications. Using assisting technology and equipment, installing wider doors, ramps, lifts, and wheelchair access, and helping people with sign language or using Braille are a few conversions that can smoothly clear up the barriers to performing day-to-day tasks.

f) Appropriate Job Allocation:

Recommending structured guidelines and relocating different job roles appropriate for a differently-abled individual will result in proficiency. For example, a visually impaired person could attend and receive phone calls or call centres. Hard-of-hearing individuals can sort out documents in the packing industry, which doesn't require verbal communication. Analysing each individual and allocating as per the guideline requirements will surely be a successful model for workplace incorporation.

g) Transportation and Accommodation:

Accommodation and transport are crucial in breaking the barrier and improving disabled employment. Americans with Disabilities Act (ADA) states that employers should provide reasonable accommodations to disabled people. The Survey of Disability and Employment 2015 shows that one-third of non-working disabled persons have reported housing and lack of transportation as employment barriers. The study conducted by Transportation-Related Challenges for Persons with Disabilities by Utah State University shows that individuals with significant disabilities face hindrance by transportation facilities.

h) Workers Benefits

The Disability Benefits Program should benefit both employers and employees mutually. The primary employer's benefits package includes a health plan and life insurance options.

In conclusion, addressing different-abled issues requires a multi-faceted approach that involves raising awareness, advocating for policy changes, and fostering a more inclusive society. Working together to overcome barriers and implement solutions can create a more equitable and supportive working environment for different-abled individuals.

(VI) SDG – Targets & Indicators	
8 DECENT WORK AND ECONOMIC GROWTH	
Target 8.5	By 2030, achieve full and productive employment and decent work for all women and men, including for young people and persons with disabilities, and equal pay for work of equal value
Indicators 8.5.1	Average hourly earnings of female and male employees, by occupation, age and persons with disabilities
Indicators 8.5.2	Unemployment rate, by sex, age and persons with disabilities
10 REDUCED INEQUALITIES	
Target 10.2	By 2030, empower and promote the social, economic and political inclusion of all, irrespective of age, sex, disability, race, ethnicity, origin, religion or economic or other status
Indicators 10.2.1	Proportion of people living below 50 per cent of median income, by age, and persons with disabilities

11 SUSTAINABLE CITIES AND COMMUNITIES	
Target 11.2	By 2030, provide access to safe, affordable, accessible and sustainable transport systems for all, improving road safety, notably by expanding public transport, with special attention to the needs of those in vulnerable situations, women, children, persons with disabilities and older persons
Indicators 11.2.1	Proportion of population that has convenient access to public transport, by sex, age and persons with disabilities
Target 11.7	By 2030, provide universal access to safe, inclusive and accessible, green and public spaces, in particular for women and children, older persons and persons with disabilities
Indicators 11.7.1	Average share of the built-up area of cities that is open space for public use for all, by sex, age and persons with disabilities

05

Abolition of Child Labour

In today's globalised world, the issue of child labour remains a pressing concern. Children around the world are being exploited in various industries, depriving them of their right to education, health, and childhood. We need to look into the complexities of child labour in the workplace and explore potential solutions for creating a more ethical and sustainable future.

Trade 4 Peace aims to raise sellers' and buyers' awareness of the need to be concerned about goods produced by enforcing child labour. Hence, we advocate improving international compliance with human rights and supporting ethical trade labelling to combat child labour.

We need to understand the root causes of the issues so that deciphering and solving them with a practical approach will be a permanent solution.

- Poverty is a fundamental driver of child labour, as families living in extreme poverty often have limited choice but to send their children to work to support the household.
- Social inequality escalates the problem, as marginalised communities are more likely to resort to child labour due to limited access to education and economic opportunities.

(I) Impacts of Child Labour

- **Physical and Mental Health Consequences**

Child labour can have severe consequences on the physical and mental health of children, exposing them to hazardous working conditions and depriving them of a normal childhood. The long hours of strenuous work and exposure to dangerous machinery can lead to injuries.

- **Education and Development**

Child labour deprives children of their right to education, trapping them in a cycle of poverty and limiting their potential for personal and societal development. Investing in education and skill development is crucial for breaking the sequence of child labour and empowering children to build a better future for themselves.

The United Nations General Assembly, Status of the Convention on the Rights of the Child, states that over 200 million children work in unfavourable conditions which violate child labour standards.

The International Labour Organization, a specialised agency for the United Nations, created checkpoints for Eliminating and Preventing Child Labour.

The 2021 World Day Against Child Labour theme is: "**Act now: end child labour.**" A recent alarming statistic told the world that we must act now to stop child labour. UNICEF and the International Labour Organization (ILO) report said that the number of children in child labour has risen to 160 million worldwide - an increase of 8.4 million children in the last four years. The COVID-19 pandemic has directly pushed millions of child labourers to the brink of poverty.

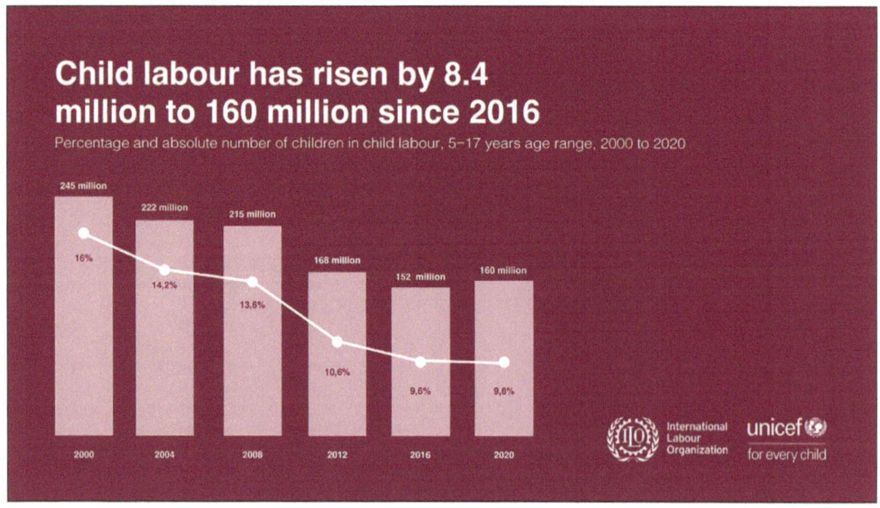

The United Nations General Assembly, Status of the Convention on the Rights of the Child, states that over 200 million children work in unfavourable conditions which violate child labour standards. The International Labour Organization, a specialised agency for the United Nations, created checkpoints for Eliminating and Preventing Child Labour.

The year 2021 is declared an International Year for the Elimination of Child Labour to empower judicial formats and solutions to obliterate Child Labour. This united resolution was formed in the United Nations General Assembly 2019 to achieve UN Sustainable Development Goals (UNSDG), Target 8.7.

Target 8.7 stipulates that the global community should take immediate and effective measures to eradicate forced labour, end modern slavery and human trafficking and secure the prohibition and elimination of the worst forms of child labour, including recruitment and use of child soldiers, and by 2025, end child labour in all its forms."

"There is no place for child labour in society. It robs children of their future and keeps families in poverty," – said ILO Director-General Guy Ryder.

According to the data, we had around 246 million in 2000 suffering from child labour and 152 million in 2016. Nearly 100 million children are rescued and removed from hardship and intense work. Even though the numbers decrease substantially, we must strive progressively to alleviate poverty. Today, around 70% of children work in farming and livestock herding under dangerous conditions for life and health.

According to ILO's Minimum Age of Convention No.138, Article 2 states; A minimum age for employment is not less than 15 years after completing compulsory schooling. Article 4 states – The minimum age for admission for work that endangers health, safety, and morals should not be less than 18 years.

(II) International Programme on the Elimination of Child Labour (IPEC) - The Worst Forms of Child Labour

"Despite impressive improvements in reducing child labour, there is still a high prevalence of child labour in Asia, with more than 62 million children trapped in child labour, of whom more than 28 million are engaged in worst forms," – said Beate Andrees, Chief of ILO's Fundamentals Principles and Rights at Work Branch (FUNDAMENTALS)

Even though we have children working under inhumane conditions in many different sectors, Child trafficking, debt bondage, child recruitment for armed conflicts, drug trafficking, pornography and prostitution are considered disasters that top the list of child labour.

We must eliminate the above forms by effectively implementing education, increasing social well-being, and rising above poverty.

Working with 26 Pathfinder countries and 240 partners, Alliance 8.7 collaborates with ILO to focus on solutions to terminate child labour practices. The top priority of Alliance 8.7 is to focus on supply chains, migration, law and judiciary, areas of conflict, and humanitarian settings.

(III) Lack of Labour Law Enforcement

- In many countries, weak enforcement of child labour laws allows businesses to exploit vulnerable children without facing consequences.
- Corruption and lack of transparency in regulatory systems further prolong the vicious cycle of child labour.

The product should be supplied and traded with human rights and standards. However, many countries' laws don't follow the same rules; in many states, child labour is an accepted reality with unfavourable working conditions and even slavery.

Currently, retailers and buyers are concerned about whether their goods were produced by enforcing child labour laws. We can combat child labour by improving international compliance with human rights and supporting ethical trade labelling.

(IV)   Forced Labour in Global Supply Chains

Child labour is child abuse. All products and services should be supplied and traded with human rights without child labour; however, many countries do not always hold the same rules. In many states, child labour is an accepted reality with unfavourable working conditions and even slavery.

Big brands produce products and services by exploiting millions of child labourers in appalling and inhumane conditions. The supply chain involves sourcing raw materials, finishing products, and retail products. Human Rights Watch has documented how the children are doing gruelling, dangerous work in cotton, coffee, garments, tobacco, sugarcane, and goldmines to supply global demand. Most products or services are engaged in small workshops or inside the home environment, making it highly challenging to identify and eradicate.

The International Labour Organization, in the report of Global Estimates 2020, Trends and the Road Forward, states that out of 200 million child labourers, 73 million children are in hazardous working conditions.

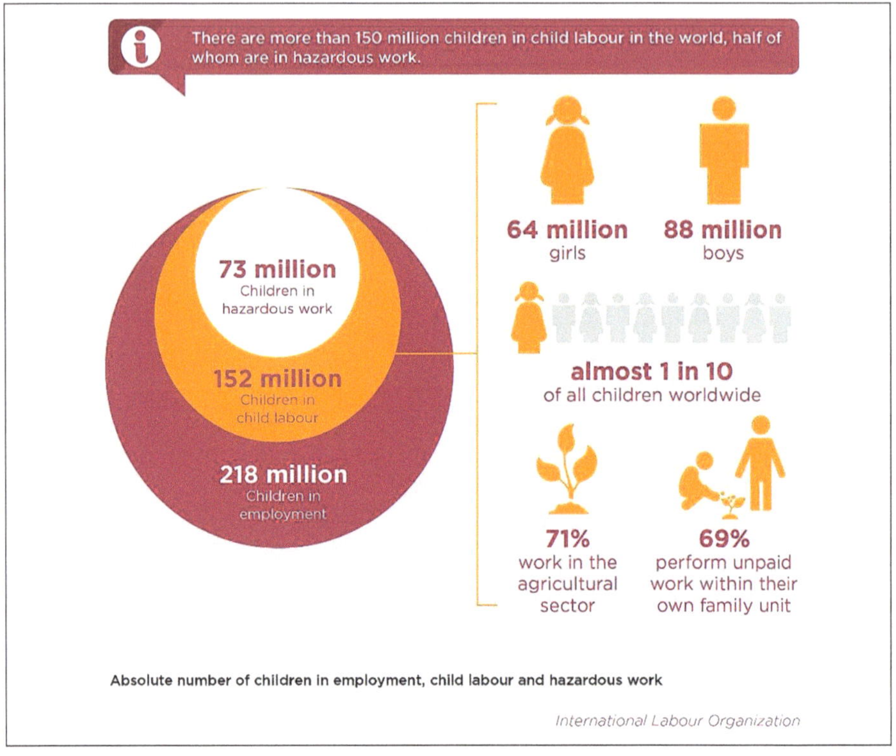

Absolute number of children in employment, child labour and hazardous work

International Labour Organization

Even though child labour exists in many industries, the textile and garment industry has the highest child labour workforce to meet ever-growing fast fashion industry consumption demands. Specific jobs like cross-pollinating, harvesting cotton, and spinning and dyeing industries prefer child labourers. The availability of a labour workforce, cheap wages, and no official supervision and unions fall under the radar and go unnoticed under this vicious process.

"Fast fashion has endangered a race to the bottom, pushing companies to find ever-cheaper sources of labour," says a UNICEF report.

(V)   Vulnerable Migrant Children

Regular migration from regions or crossing national borders through legal or irregular transit channels increases the exposure to abuse and exploitation of migrant children. The children who the migrant parents leave behind are vulnerable to human trafficking. Among child labour, migrant children are at high risk of exploitation due to the absence of legal child protection and effective policies to support them legally. Undocumented migrant children are often sent to detention centres, and inadequate education and healthcare in the centres make the children more vulnerable.

The political turmoil and civil unrest forced mass migration from various countries to seek asylum in developed countries. The situation conceived new projects to focus on migrant children and collaboration with different international organisations and NGOs to promote inclusion in society.

International Programme on the Elimination of Child Labour (IPEC), article 5, states, "Government should consider ways to address the potential vulnerability of children to, in particular, the worst forms of child labour, in the context of migratory flows."

(VI)   Breaking the Vicious Cycle

a) Implementing Regulations

With the onset of social awareness, various government advisory bodies and organisations have taken stringent measures and checkpoints to monitor legislation's transformation and development. According to the Organisation for Economic Co-operation and Development (OECD), 28-43% of Child labour indirectly contributes to the supply chain of exports worldwide.

Government and non-governmental institutions should raise awareness of the adverse effects of forced labour while incorporating policies. The majority of child labour employment is found in the private sector, making it hard to track and eliminate them.

The essence of the Australian Senate's Modern Slavery Act 2018, United Kingdom's Modern Slavery Act 2015, France's Duty of Vigilance Law

2017 and California's Transparency in Supply Chains Act 2010 – is for businesses to take stringent action on supply chain practices.

Many countries share the strategic vision of striving for a common approach to innovative measures and ethical supply chain practices.

The British government is a pioneer in combating modern slavery by taking extreme measures against traffickers and coercion businesses to scrutinise supply chains for abuse and free from child labour. The recent UK-Germany Joint Declaration, June 2021, promotes joint efforts to end child labour and forced labour and nurture responsibility in supply chains as a collective global responsibility of commitment to society.

The Government of Canada has taken tremendous initiative towards the companies to take relevant action against child labour, modern slavery, and human rights violations. Over 50,000 Canadians have signed the petition to voice their support for supply chain legislation, and 91% favour taking the positive step, says Executive Director of Fairtrade Canada, Julie Francoeur. NGOs and various organisations must collaborate with the government to share and contribute their expertise to support the legislation.

Even though governments are stepping up to curb child labour and enforce necessary laws aimed at businesses, we must take civilised action as responsible citizens and consumers.

b) Corporate Responsibility

Many businesses recognise the adverse effects caused by the role of supply chains in the intake of child labour and rectify this by taking appropriate measures.

The extensive use of child labour in West Africa's cocoa industry has led to the initiation of a slave-free norm in making chocolate, which is an incredible movement. While few companies take resolutions by committing to source responsibly, many large brands still refuse to guarantee that their chocolate is produced free from child labour.

Even though many labels are on chocolate bars with various Fair Trade certifications and Rain Forest Alliance Certification, none guarantees that chocolate is made with exploitive child labour. We need concrete labelling in the products and services to ensure that the goods are child labour-free.

From eyeshadows to lipsticks, mica is a listed ingredient in many cosmetics. Around 60% of the world's mica comes from illegal mining in India. The shimmering dark secret in the make-up industry traces its origins to child labour. The children illegally mine the mica, a natural mineral, as the small stature can easily access the narrow, compact mine shafts. The children do not have access to education and also face hazardous health defects. While many companies do not declare mica's source, a few brands navigate the complicated issue and use synthetic mica or ethically sourced.

Brands must address this issue, take action, and look into unethical child labour in their supply chain. Consumers' preferences are inclined towards the goods produced being environmentally friendly, ethically sourced, and socially responsible.

c) Social & Ethical Initiatives

Trade 4 Peace aims to bring responsible consumers who refuse to buy the products from companies and insist on the framework; these guidelines enforce ethical practices and stringent licences to accelerate the elimination of forced labour and human trafficking. Trade 4 Peace is choosing to support companies with ethical sourcing and accreditation with labels with Fair Trade so we can all be responsible consumers to break down the cycle of child labour and poverty.

Various accreditations like Fair Trade and Child Labour Free are working relentlessly towards eradicating child labour. Like the Trade 4 Peace accreditation model, we must initiate ethical and social standards across individuals and organisations to eliminate child labour.

The Trade 4 Peace's main objectives are to offer realistic solutions to the global economy by refraining from underage employment, which will help world trade and promote children's education. Offering realistic solutions such as refraining from underage employment will not only help in terms of trade but also provide a chance for the children to get an education.

Eradicating child labour in the workplace requires a multi-faceted approach to address the root cause and promote sustainable solutions. By strengthening legal frameworks, investing in education, and fostering collaboration, we can create a future where children are protected from exploitation and have the opportunity to thrive. We can build a more just and equitable society for future generations.

(VII) SDG – Targets & Indicators	
8 DECENT WORK AND ECONOMIC GROWTH	
Target 8.7	Take immediate and effective measures to eradicate forced labour, end modern slavery and human trafficking and secure the prohibition and elimination of the worst forms of child labour, including recruitment and use of child soldiers, and by 2025 end child labour in all its forms
Indicators 8.7.1	Proportion and number of children aged 5-17 years engaged in child labour, by sex and age
16 PEACE, JUSTICE AND STRONG INSTITUTIONS	
Target 16.2	End abuse, exploitation, trafficking and all forms of violence and torture against children

Diversity, Equity & Inclusion

Diversity, Equity & Inclusion have become crucial topics in the workplace globally. Organisations realise the significance of having a diverse workforce from talent pools from all categories. We must explore the need for a diversified workforce, the issues that can arise and prospective solutions to create an inclusive working environment.

External social influences stigmatise people from various races, ethnic and religions. Rather than evaluating, we should understand the concept of tolerance without any prejudice, as it limits our ability to assess, create and develop further.

(I)   Significance of Diversity, Equity & Inclusion

For the past few decades, the management of cultural and religious diversity has become a prominent narrative as there is a high rise in global displacement and immigration. With diversified globalisation and migration, we have minority groups in our society. Businesses need talented workers belonging to diverse communities. By adapting and embracing multicultural intergroups, we can utilise our talents and reinvent ourselves with peaceful coexistence.

Inclusion is stated as embracing all-in-one ideology irrespective of gender, race, age, religious and cultural differences without barriers and discrimination. It is about giving opportunities to be involved equally without intolerance.

The primary focus of inclusion is to alter the necessary adjustments and provide apt circumstances to adapt to individual needs. To create and establish connections and respect between multicultural and inclusive workforces.

Hate crimes against minorities give us a rare chance to look into a new perspective. Dialogues around DE&I have risen recently, creating a resurgence in many organisations. The businesses started by doubling the measures in diversity metrics like hiring, job retention and utilisation of multi-talented resources.

If we look at the prosperous countries and economic urban centres like Dubai, Singapore, and New York – they have the highest percentage of immigrants. Immigrants are proportionate innovation, which is a crucial factor in economic performance. The 2016 report by Weber Shandwick shows that 47% of job seekers opt for a diverse organisation.

It is imperative to establish the concept of DE&I to allow and materialise in the organisation. Our primary goal is to create a working environment with plurality and equal opportunities for all. The corporate policies and internal regulations should be aligned, complemented and prioritised at the fundamental level for practical implementation.

In a broad sense, respect individuals, equal opportunities and rights, no prejudices, and connect all human beings irrespective of differences.

(II)   Focus for DE&I

We live in a very different time, with a lot of movements, global displacement, and extensive political changes, and these things bring us to see a closer look at multicultural ethnic groups, gender disparity, minority groups and racism.

The place we live, our neighbourhood, our schools, the places we shop, our friends, and our social circles all consist of different cultures and ethnicities. In our everyday lives, we meet and communicate with various cultures of different ages, sexual orientations, genders, and races. So, it makes it fair for us to embrace the same in work culture.

Even though everyone knows the workplace should be diverse, implementing them comes under many checkpoints. It does not only benefit the business, but it's also the right thing to do. The diverse backgrounds and experiences are a creative hub for many innovations and solving problems. People tend to join companies and organisations with a diverse environment as they will comfortably fit in. A study from Josh Bersin says the diversity of inclusive organisations generates 2.3 times more cash flow per employee and 120 % to meet the target.

a) Pandemic Response

The Covid pandemic remodelled our way of thinking from different perspectives. The leaders and employees are becoming aware of inequalities in the workplace highlighted by COVID-19. Catalyst surveyed 1,100 working adults from 250 business leaders and 850 employees from full-time employment of various races, ages, genders and ethnicities. This report revealed that even though the employees are uncertain and aware that their company is keen to create an inclusive work environment, they are confident about diversity and an inclusive workplace in the aftermath of the Covid pandemic. Five out of 10 working people anticipate the acceleration of better prospects, and 7 out of 10 people assume that the workplace will steer towards an inclusive work culture.

This Covid has brought many issues to the surface, and many opportunities have been created to address the gender and race disparities and stratagem towards equity and inclusion. The new normal of working from home, flexible working hours, and conducting online meetings have given equal opportunities to everyone. Remote work facilitates no gender disparity; performed tasks are assessed only on results. However, remote working has shown that 21% of women are overlooked than 15% of men during virtual meetings. When questioned about the racial and ethnic inequalities tackled by their company, 65% of business leaders acknowledged execution, and 56% of employees disagreed with the motion.

An estimated average of 41%, 39% of women, and 45% of men acknowledged their company is committed to building an inclusive work environment.

(III)   DE&I Progression

Diversifying talents is essential for developing innovation, creativity, and good decision-making in the workplace. When people from different cultures and environments join, they can bring exclusive vantage perspectives and out-of-box ideas to the organisation. It is a fundamental humane quality to ensure that all employees are treated and given equal opportunities to succeed.

The World Economic Forum, Boston Consulting Group Study reports that a diverse organisation generates 19% financial gain due to various innovative talent pools.

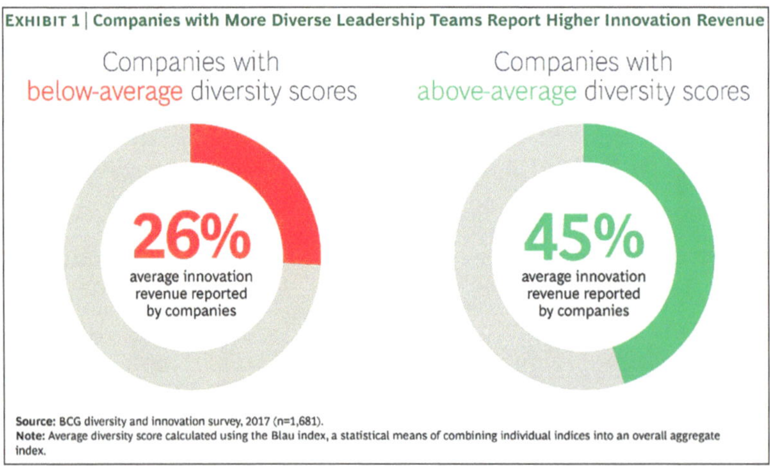

We live in a world of many different ethnicities and cultures, and the workplace should exhibit a broad spectrum of diversity and variety.

Our primary goal is to create a work environment that strengthens and allows Diversity & Inclusion in all areas of age, gender, ethnicity, race, culture, religion, disability, and special needs to imbibe into the work culture.

The approach of DE&I in the workplace is changing and evolving immensely. Multicultural diversity doesn't refer to solely diverse cultures but also includes everyone irrespective of age, gender, specially-abled and converging as human-centric engagement.

a) Instil and strengthen DE&I

Regardless of growing acknowledgement and the significance of DE&I, many organisations still face challenges in this sector. Common issues such as discrimination, preconceived notions, bias, and lack of representation are a few obstacles that can occur. These unconscious biases can lead to partiality in hiring, promotion and conduct towards the employees.

Creating awareness by inspiring personal interactions and supporting focus groups and sessions makes a lasting impression and change on personal levels. The personal experiences faced by each person will focus on the problems in the limelight. Societal changes unquestionably affect the economy, creating individuals, professionals, and organisations who realise the importance of diversity and inclusion in civil society, which is pivotal. Integrating diverse cultures, knowledge, experience and skills in the workforce in recruiting and development will enhance the company's progress.

- Equal opportunities will boost morale and result in less attrition.
- Raising awareness of diversity and understanding from different perspectives

- Creating mentorship programmes and employee resource groups to include a sense of support for underrepresented groups
- Implementing policies and strategies to promote fairness and equality in the workforce.
- Addressing key points such as pay disparities, promotion opportunities, and flexible work timings equally for all employees.
- An inclusive work culture provides an equal platform for all, irrespective of age, gender, disability or special needs.

We can achieve all the above by integrating human values and being socially responsible to create a harmonious workplace.

b) Integration of Cultural Importance

The International Fund for Cultural Diversity (IFCD) by UNESCO is a multi-donor fund for promoting Diversity and Cultural Expressions - article 18, 2005 by conducting various projects and supporting organisations to nurture and converge multiple cultures.

These reinforcement activities and strategies will boost cultural entrepreneurs and institutions promoting cultural activities and sprout the growth of cultural business industries. The perception and mindfulness of living together with various multicultural sectors is crucial to living in harmony.

c) Recruitment & Promotion

Recruitment must be objective and unbiased to reduce attrition and job retention. HR professionals should focus on recruiting diverse employees. What is diversity in the workplace? It is the coexistence of age, race, and gender that causes different races to converge together. We cannot have diverse forces without inclusion. Employees should feel equal opportunities in hiring, training and promotions.

When selecting an employee, apart from the experience required for a particular task, critical thinking, out-of-box ideas, and multi-tasking are crucial attributes. It is high time we incorporate these qualities in recruitment. It is undebatable to acknowledge skill shortage; it is phenomenal, and diversified talents will curb the problems. Even though the numbers have decreased, we still have a long way to go before achieving and implementing our goal. We need to select from a broader talent resource to fill the gaps. Problem-solving with multitudes of perspectives from various backgrounds will bring the utmost benefit of box innovative ideas and consensus-building.

All it takes is immense afresh thinking when they're recruiting. Simply fulfilling the numbers that qualify for a diverse team is not sufficient. The quality of the people with different perspectives and diverse vantage points will bring out new ideas. Relying solely on the right qualifications and impressive backgrounds with experience might not give us exact outcomes. Hands-on experience, field knowledge, wide-ranging interest, and problem-solving in complex and unpredictable situations exemplify a diverse workforce. A well-diverse distributed company tends to think differently and can get beyond the usual way of getting things done.

Transforming words into action is a proactive way to include a creative, equal environment. The hiring process, internal training promotions, equal pay and employee programmes will retain the employees.

We must monitor human resources and guide companies in forming a strategy to embrace diversity and inclusion under employee resource groups (ERGs). The auditing of equality pays analysis throughout the organisation.

A diversity and inclusive council should be formed to support Indigenous, minority communities, LGBTQ, and other priority groups in strategically implementing appointments, training programmes, and other organisational processes. To support and uplift talented individuals irrespective of age, gender and racial disparities and honour them will acknowledge their career advancement and boost their morale. Prioritising people and workplace belonging increases performance and reduces job attrition.

The parental leave policy should be gender-neutral to aid and facilitate all equally. Regular monitoring of gender evaluation and checkpoints should be tied up to performance goals and internal two-way feedback to managers.

These tangible solutions create a positive trajectory to accelerate equity and diversity inclusion in the workforce. When we live all life homogeneously, implementing the same in the workplace will be relatively more straightforward and identical. When we have a diverse workforce, recreating equal opportunity and discrimination is a moral value and an asset to the company. The progress toward equality is progress for humanity.

(IV) Management of Diversity - Four Paradigms

Implementing diversity in the workforce requires many drastic changes, starting from recruitment and workflow, but not without fuelling tensions. We must encourage an amicable work environment with functional groups from different cultural backgrounds without predominance and oppression. Any indifferences should be handled sensitively and resolved carefully to maintain a diverse workforce.

We can broadly classify it into four major paradigms in managing diversity.

a) Resistance Paradigm

Employees resist organisational change and reject any new practices from management, leading to significant inequality in the workforce. Any societal changes, whether the development of new ideas, are always met with disapproval first. Our deep-seated beliefs and ideas are not easily changed, and when presented with new methods, they are always met with resistance to change. The changes can be incorporated into the workforce by encouraging new implementation, and supporting the change will result in positive organisational change.

b) Discrimination & Fairness Paradigm

The equal and fair treatment of the workforce is affiliated with EEO (Equal opportunity) guidelines, and it can be implemented by recruiting socially vulnerable minority groups and streamlining across all fields in the work process. Even though the recruitment of diverse forces, treating everyone equally and embracing the difference is a humongous task. Any job requires qualifications and experience, and despite meeting them, it would be fitting to qualify for the job and not reject the applicants just because they are not suitable for, e.g., women, minority groups, age, etc., as long it is specifically required for the job. Any indifferences and biased practices will breed discontent towards the management.

c) Access – Legitimacy Paradigm

It is one of the popular paradigms, and organisations use this theory and implement it to capture specific demographic markets. The organisation's diverse workforce gives the trust to lure the market, which is otherwise resilient to decode. In practice, people are more comfortable dealing with people who resemble them. Entering a new country or tapping into a new demographic will be much easier when similar cultural and ethnic knowledge is utilised for business expansion. The partnerships, distributors, customised products, and legal issues can be easily managed with appropriate local knowledge.

d) Learning & Effectiveness Paradigm

Training, coaching and career management should be dispersed among all the employees. Promotions and appraisals are to be evaluated with no comprehension and with 360 performance reports. The freedom of expression and work-related ideas will be a great asset. Any constructive changes and openness to new discussions are the keys to the transition to the learning paradigm.

(V) Implementation of Checkpoints

Organisations need to fully embrace the concept of diverse hires from functional and ethical views to tap the broad angle of the talent pool spectrum. Organisations attempt to implement corporate social responsibility (CSR) and engage in humanistic values for social accountability.

Companies with more than 15 employees must follow equal employment opportunity(EEO), a regulatory body that imposes diversity in the workforce. The following laws and guidelines have the authority over any discriminatory workplace practices.

- Title VII of the Civil Rights Act of 1964
- The Equal Pay Act of 1963 (EPA)
- The age discrimination in employment act of 1967 (ADEA)
- Title 1 Americans with Disabilities Act of 1990 (ADA)
- The genetic information non-discrimination act of 2008 (GINA)

The Equal Employment Opportunity Commission [EEOC] has made the survey guidelines for the company's operations. These reports are submitted annually and are categorised by age, gender, race, and job category. Apart from submitting the EEO report, the EEOC also emphasised equal opportunity employer statements in the job advertisement.

Stating that the organisation is an opportunity employer and against non-discriminatory action in the workforce will ensure many responses from various groups. The simple declaration of ads and filling the report is a good starting point to attract multiple talents, and the intention should be achieved in a continued work environment.

But why EEO law is essential? Why should we stress implementation in organisations? Whether a diverse workforce is the right thing to do, what do we gain anything from it? It is both. We have different backgrounds and ethnic races, and these differences have nothing to do with performing the job. Equality in the workplace goes beyond the guidelines and laws and ensures neutralism overall in employment. Even though we have rules and procedures in place for companies to oblige, it is our moral duty and ethics to reflect a better society.

Diverse ideas with different perspectives bring solutions than homogeneous teams. We must charter and utilise this talent pool without bias for better achievement. For the past few decades, the management of cultural and religious diversity has become a prominent narrative as there is a high rise in global displacement and immigration.

With diversified globalisation and migration, we have minority groups in our society. Businesses need talented workers belonging to diverse communities. By adapting and embracing multicultural intergroups, we can utilise our talents and reinvent ourselves with peaceful coexistence.

External social influences stigmatise people from various races, ethnic, and religions. Rather than evaluating, we should understand the concept of tolerance without any prejudice, as it limits our ability to assess, create, and develop further.

By fostering an inclusive workplace, companies can tap into diverse talent, promote creativity, and better serve their increasingly diverse customer base. The path to progress may not be easy, but the rewards of a truly inclusive organisation are immeasurable.

Achieving genuine diversity and inclusion needs a multi-prong approach. The initiatives should not be at the surface level, but day-to-day operations issues must be addressed to prevent the barriers. When management observes the problems of a diverse workforce, practical solutions will be commenced to empower them. These approaches can create a more positive and productive working environment by actively boosting the DE&I in the workplace, where all employees feel valued, respected, and treated equally. The progressive path may not be easy-going, but the benefits of the diversified organisation are infinite.

(VI) SDG – Targets & Indicators	
10 REDUCED INEQUALITIES	
Target 10.2	By 2030, empower and promote the social, economic and political inclusion of all, irrespective of age, sex, disability, race, ethnicity, origin, religion or economic or other status
Indicators 10.2.1	Proportion of people living below 50 per cent of median income, by age, and persons with disabilities
Target 10.3	Ensure equal opportunity and reduce inequalities of outcome, including by eliminating discriminatory laws, policies and practices and promoting appropriate legislation, policies and action in this regard
Indicators 10.3.1	Proportion of the population reporting having personally felt discriminated against or harassed within the previous 12 months on the basis of a ground of discrimination prohibited under international human rights law
5 GENDER EQUALITY	
Target 5.1	End all forms of discrimination against all women and girls everywhere

Indicators 5.1.1	Whether or not legal frameworks are in place to promote, enforce and monitor equality and non-discrimination on the basis of sex
Target 5.5	Ensure women's full and effective participation and equal opportunities for leadership at all levels of decision-making in political, economic and public life
Indicators 5.5.2	Proportion of women in managerial positions
8 DECENT WORK AND ECONOMIC GROWTH	
Target 8.2	Achieve higher levels of economic productivity through diversification, technological upgrading and innovation, including through a focus on high-value added and labour-intensive sectors
Indicators 8.2.1	Annual growth rate of real GDP per employed person

07

Basic Human Rights

Imagine a world where everyone is entitled to basic human rights, which forms the foundation of an equally fair and just society. We need to explore what they entail and why they are crucial for the well-being of individuals and society.

Basic human rights are the fundamental rights for all humans irrespective of race, gender, ethnicity, nationality, or religion. The concept of basic human rights reflects a shared belief in the inherent worth and dignity of every human being, irrespective of external characteristics or circumstances.

The United Nations General Assembly (UNGA) implemented the Universal Declaration of Human Rights (UDHR) in 1948. This declaration commemorates all human beings' basic, civil, political, economic, social and cultural rights.

The UDHR, in unison with the International Covenant on Civil and Political Rights and the International Covenant on Economic, Social and Cultural Rights, forms the International Bill for Human Rights.

The quantitative, qualitative, subjective, and objective indicators are developed to cover all civil, political, economic, social, and cultural rights, respectively. Complying with the International Human Rights Treaties, the governments are equipped with domestic measures and legislation obligations. Upon failure to comply and address basic human rights abuse, the procedures are available at regional and international points to ensure the protection of basic human rights standards.

Human rights encompass many rights, including life, liberty, security, equality, and dignity. Basic human rights are universal, inalienable, and indivisible.

(I)   Global Efforts for Basic Human Rights

The international human rights framework, encompassing treaties, conventions, and monitoring mechanisms, is pivotal in promoting and protecting basic human rights worldwide. Bodies like the United Nations Human Rights Council and regional human rights courts work towards ensuring compliance with human rights standards.

The idea of basic human rights has its roots in various historical documents and philosophical traditions. One of the most significant milestones in recognising human rights is the Universal Declaration of Human Rights, adopted by the United Nations General Assembly in 1948.

The United Nations Human Rights Commission established the 'Universal Declaration of Human Rights' (UDHR) under the chairmanship of Eleanor Roosevelt. The Declaration is the most universal human right documented by the representatives of all regions. Even though there are many traits for basic human rights, the United for Human Rights (UHR) has filed the basic 30 human rights.

By the ILO Convention C39 (1930), The Forced Labour Convention, C105 (1957) Abolition of Forced Labour Convention, C190 (2019) Violence & Harassment Conventions, any form of racial, social, religious discrimination, abuse and sexual harassment, forced labour extraction will have a consequence of penalty and criminal conviction. These frameworks promote healthier and mutual growth in the business.

According to the World Economic Forum (WEF) report, around 43 billion people are exploited by forced labour and debt-bonded labour globally.

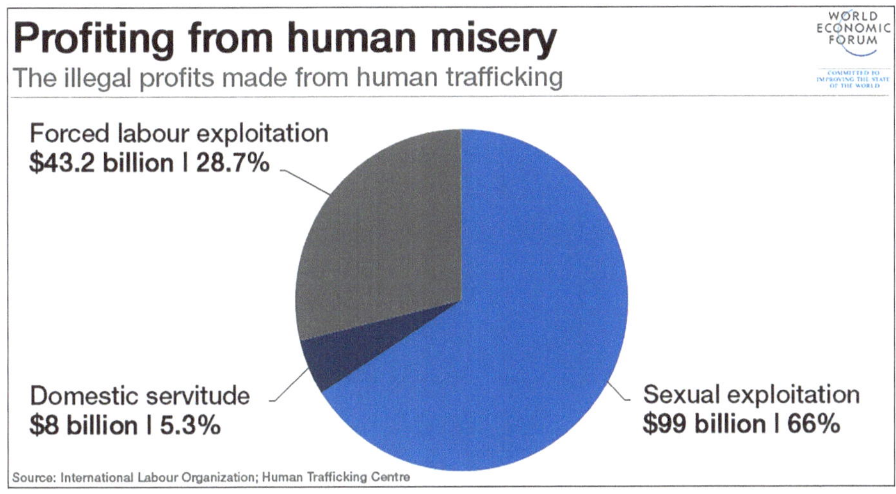

Grassroots movements, civil society organisations, and human rights defenders play a significant role in advocating for basic human rights at the local, national, and international levels. Globally, the advocators of human rights are primarily citizens, and particularly (NGOs) monitor the execution of human rights implementation by the governments. Their efforts raise awareness, hold governments accountable, and bring positive change.

(II)   Scope of the Effect

a) Right to Equality

Prohibition of discrimination based on gender, sexual orientation, race and religious beliefs. The equality law obliges employers to reasonably adapt to persons with special needs in the working environment. It is essential to uphold the dignity and worth of every individual to ensure that no one is subjected to unjustified treatment and treated with respect and equality.

b) Right to Equality in Recruitment

Organisations should not discriminate against potential employees based on gender or minority candidates. In some countries, organisations have introduced anonymous applications without names. This method helps black and ethnic minorities (BAME) candidates to secure more jobs.

c) Equal Pay

According to the International Covenant on Economic, Social and Cultural Rights Article 7, organisations must pay sufficient minimum wage to support families. Companies are held accountable for unfair pay and improper working conditions.

When two people perform equivalent jobs, then the pay should be equal. But in reality, women are paid less than men.

d) Maternity Rights

Women have the right to return to the same job and the position after the maternity leave. It is unlawful discrimination if any training or chance of promotion is missed due to maternity leave. Women are most likely to suffer because of the diminished legal protection.

e) Protection Against Sexual Harassment

When an individual engages with the intention of knowingly or unconsciously violating privacy, either physically or emotionally, the employers are obliged to take action either by management rights or by legal means. The employers are accountable for creating a safe and sexual harassment-free zone for the employees.

f) Respect for Religious Beliefs

The Freedom of Religion, by Article 18 of the Universal Declaration on Human Rights (UDHR) and European Convention on Human Rights Article 9 –states that everyone has the right to freedom of thought, conscience and religion; this right includes freedom to change his religion or belief and freedom. This is subjected to marginal adjustments in an organisation with reasonable limitations.

(III)   Key Issues

The International Labour Conference, report of 'Fundamental principles and rights at work: From challenges to opportunities':

a) Freedom of Association

Employers and workers have the right to join organisations of their interest. The Committee on Freedom of Association has evaluated cases from 77 countries, revealing that half of the cases involved anti-union discrimination. The International Trade Union Confederation (ITUC) has facts containing violations of worker's rights, protests and imprisonment. The 2016 UN Special Rapporteur suggests that states should avoid anti-union policies and create an optimal environment to exercise the rights of freedom of association in the workplace.

b) Inequality of Wages

The Minimum Wage Fixing Convention of 1970 determined that the minimum wage should comply with national and social elements. This plays a significant role in fixing minimum wages, which will curb the widening of financial inequality.

c) Elimination of Forced Labour

All forms of slavery, such as bondage work, underage employment, and human trafficking, are severe cases of human rights violation. Immigrants, underage children, and minority indigenous people are the most affected. The International Labour Organization (ILO) published in a report that 21 million people are under the forced labour category, including 5.5 million children. Most of the forced labour is often unseen by the public in mining, fishing vessels, alley workshops, and plantations.

The International Labour Organization (ILO), Walk Free, and International Organization of Migration (IOM) have estimated around 50 million people are struggling under the Global Survey Index (GSI).

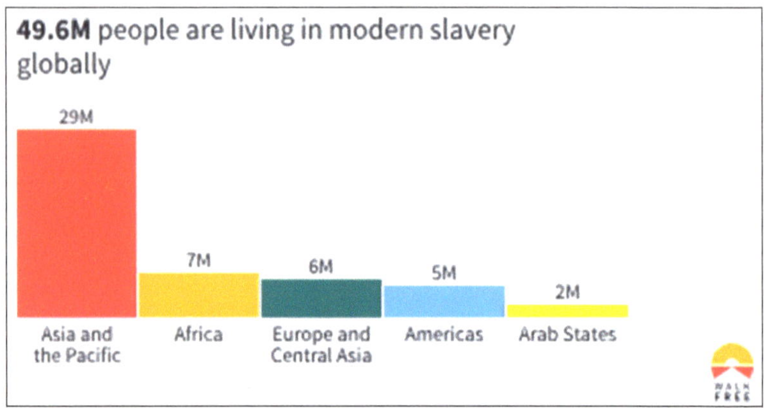

(IV)　Challenges of Application

Despite the array of constitutional and legal provisions for the protection and implementation of human rights, there are persistent issues of religion, caste, gender discrimination, and exploitation of immigrant and minority groups.

A United Nations' Report presents a synopsis of the causes of the violation of human rights, included therein:

- Poverty & Global inequalities
- Discrimination
- Armed conflict and violence
- Impunity
- Democracy deficits
- Weak institutions

a) Implementation Objections

1. The Knowledge Gap
2. The Capacity Gap
3. The Commitment Gap
4. The Security Gap

The basic notion of human rights is how we live and work; however, the workplace often presents challenges when upholding these rights. The employees may face countless obstacles which hinder their ability to showcase their talents in the working environment. We need to curb the liabilities and navigate these issues effectively.

b) Identifying Microaggressions

It refers to the subtle, often unintentional comments or behaviours that suggest discriminatory attributes. Stereotyping, exclusion, and prejudice are a few forms resulting from preconceived notions. We need to understand and address microaggressions to nurture an inclusive workplace.

c) Prevailing Bias

It is a prevalent issue in many organisations, indirectly influencing decisions linked to recruitment and promotions. We can create a healthy, equitable work environment by boosting awareness and implementing policies to mitigate unconscious bias.

d) Fundamental Rights

Safeguarding and respecting employees' personal information and data privacy protection. Access to a safe and harassment-free environment. Empowering employees to advocate freedom of association and interest is crucial to the solution.

e) Supportive Strategies

The interdisciplinary approach involving the policymakers, management, and employee feedback is the practical approach to fostering workable solutions.

(V)   Implementation of Solutions

a) Right to choose

The policy framework dialogues between employers and workers are crucial to enable the freedom of association. Strengthening employment regulations will have a minimal impact on the issue.

b) Legal Support

Many countries have amended the legal framework and legislation to support forced labour and human trafficking—the labour inspection with the particular task units to supervise the breach of the enforcement. Mutual collaboration between the labour inspection and the local public institutions will effectively exchange information and action.

Many countries have revised the legal framework at national and regional levels to strengthen a total of 194 laws. Nearly 30 countries have embraced the 'Domestic Workers Convention of 2011, practising policies for legal protection to deter forced labour.

c) Social Benefits

The socio-economic security and fundamental work for adults with appropriate wages will reduce the chances of bonded or underage working. Education and social protection are the key parameters relevant to the decrease in child labour. Immediate recovery from political or conflict-driven areas and action to protect vulnerable children directly affect underage labour. Separating children from armed conflict groups and re-integrating them back into society by programmes.

Basic human rights are the cornerstone of a just and equitable society. By recognising and upholding these rights, we can create a world where everyone is treated with dignity, respect, and fairness. Only by prioritising basic human rights can we build workplaces that respect all. We must continue to uphold and defend basic human rights for the well-being and prosperity of all. As we navigate the complexities of basic human rights challenges in the workplace, it is crucial to prioritise fairness, equality, and inclusivity.

We need to prioritise equality and inclusivity as we plan around the working model for human rights challenges. By distinguishing and managing discrimination and providing fair treatment in a supportive environment, organisations and employees can formulate a workplace where everyone is treated equally. Let us strive to build a prospective future where basic human rights are upheld in all spheres of the workforce.

"Human rights are not a privilege conferred by government. They are every human being's entitlement by virtue of his humanity." – Mother Teresa.

(VI) SDG – Targets & Indicators	
8 DECENT WORK AND ECONOMIC GROWTH	
Target 8.8	Protect labour rights and promote safe and secure working environment for all workers, including migrant workers, in particular woman migrants, and those in precarious employment
Indicators 8.8.1	Fatal and non-fatal occupational injuries per 100,000 workers, by sex and migrant status
Indicators 8.8.2	Level of national compliance with labour rights (freedom of association and collective bargaining) based on International Labour Organization (ILO) textual sources and national legislation, by sex and migrant status
10 REDUCED INEQUALITIES	
Target 10.3	Ensure equal opportunity and reduce inequalities of outcome, including by eliminating discriminatory laws, policies and practices and promoting appropriate legislation, policies and action in this regard

Indicators 10.3.1	Proportion of the population reporting having personally felt discriminated against or harassed within the previous 12 months on the basis of a ground of discrimination prohibited under international human rights law
Target 10.4	Adopt policies, especially fiscal, wage and social protection policies, and progressively achieve greater equality
Indicators 10.4.1	Labour share of GDP
Indicators 10.4.2	Redistributive impact of fiscal policy

08

Environmental Responsibility

Environmental responsibility refers to the essential pact for individuals and organisations to preserve the environment and promote sustainable practices. The impact of human interaction on the environment has become increasingly apparent, leading to pollution, climate change and loss of biodiversity.

There is a massive demand for utilisation and consumerism, which increases production scale and adversely affects the environment. The primary focus of government environmental policy is to minimise the environmental impact caused by businesses.

Protecting and preserving the environment and sustainable development are the World Trade Organization's fundamental (WTO) goals. It ensures the above targets through its rules and enforcement through WTO bodies. The World Health Organization (WHO) estimates that around 90% of the population breathes polluted air.

The UN Environment Programme Annual Report 2023 highlights the key points below:

- 42% of the world needs to cut down on greenhouse gas emissions by 2030 to limit 1.5 °C.
- One hundred thirty-eight countries are supporting the UNEP and UNDP in safeguarding biodiversity.

The United Nations body for assessing climate change, the Intergovernmental Panel on Climate Change (IPCC), has a special report that claims the negative impact of global warming is due to the increase of 1.5 °C.

As humans, we are responsible for promoting economic and sustainable development. We must channel our energy and focus in an environmentally accountable direction to achieve this. The effects of environmental pollution will not be borne only by the creators but also will affect society.

(I)   Environmental Degradation Causes

a) Human Interference

The primary cause of environmental degradation is the unsustainable practices embraced by humans. The excessive use of natural resources, encroachment, deforestation, and overconsumption have led to the global depletion of the natural environment.

b) Industrialisation

The rapid pace of industrialisation has adversely contributed to environmental declination. Industries release harmful emissions into the atmosphere, pollute water bodies, and generate large amounts of inadequate recycled wastage before disposal.

The UN Environment Programme Emission Gap Report shows the countries which are the major contributors to global warming.

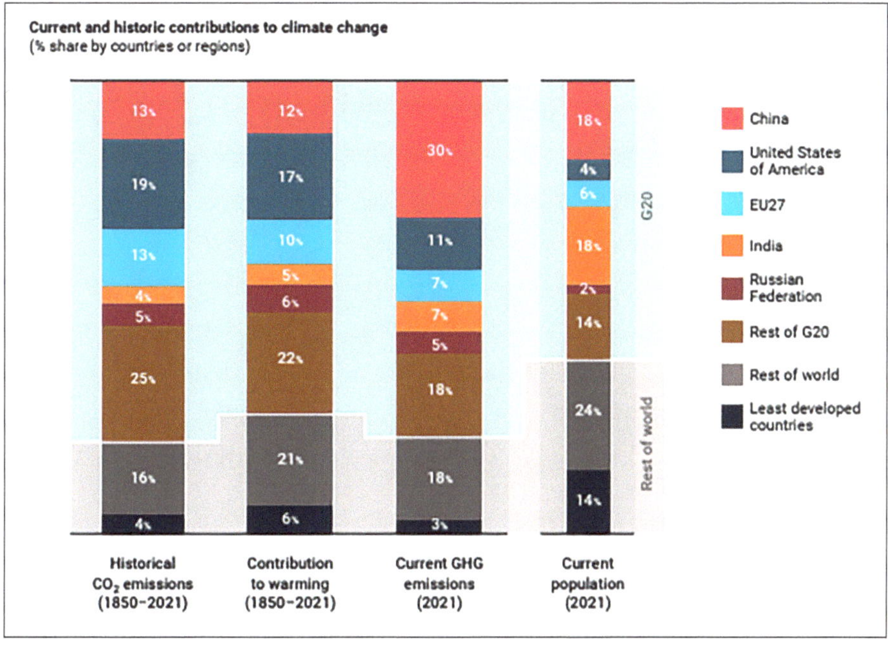

c) Deforestation

Deforestation is caused by the excessive demand for agricultural land and urban expansion, significantly impacting the environment. Waste disposal, landfills, and toxic gases lead to the loss of biodiversity, disruption of ecosystems, and climate change.

(II)   Negligence of Responsibility

a) Climate Change

Climate change is one of the most pressing issues associated with environmental irresponsibility. Global warming and unpredictable weather patterns are caused by the burning of fossil fuels, deforestation, and industrial operations, which have amplified the concentration of greenhouse gases in the atmosphere,

b) Pollution

Whether air, water, or land pollution severely threatens the environment and human health and well-being. Industrial emissions, landfills, and chemical pollutants contaminate the environment by affecting ecosystems and endanger wildlife.

c) Loss of Biodiversity

The overexploitation of natural resources and the destruction of natural habitats has led to significant biodiversity loss worldwide. The balance of ecosystems is threatened due to human interference, causing the extinction of endangered species and the planet's well-being.

(III)   Societal Commitment

A business's social responsibility is to protect and promote the natural environment and sustainability. While industrial growth is foremost for economic development, it is also imperative to see the ramifications of climatic change on the planet. We need to find the right balance to incorporate natural and sustainable practices and offset any imbalance created.

Using Natural resources, reducing the negative impact on the environment, Conservation of energy, and Waste & Effluent management are a few of the areas to focus primarily.

a) Corporate Social Responsibility (CSR)

Companies and brands must adopt and maintain sustainable practices as a central focal point to meet customer needs. Corporate companies have understood that negligence of the environment is not in practice anymore. Beyond the business, it is not only duty compiled to legal but also moral and social responsibility.

The financial strategy for a company's growth is to capitalise on the maximum profits and minimise operational costs. Earlier, the strategy goals ended here, but now we have purpose-driven Chief

Executive Officers and Leaders who commit to making business more environmentally friendly to bring about positive change, thereby increasing financial performance. An international report study by Unil indicates that a third of consumers (33%) prefer brands that contribute to society and the environment. This shows the imperative action to go beyond the conventional focus of sales, profits, affordability and improvements in social and environmental practices. Giant corporations do not recognise social responsibility, and all businesses, whether large or small, can contribute to reducing their carbon footprint.

Many companies want to capture and contribute to the social and environment-conscious market, but how many companies incorporate it into their business model? Environmental responsibility is the pivotal focus when it comes to social responsibility.

b) Sustainable Brand Index

It is one of Europe's most prominent brand studies on sustainability, with 1500 brands and 35 industries spanning eight countries. The brands measured sustainability. The Sustainability Brand Index 2021 report indicates that 68-74% of Nordic customers are inclined to choose products tagged with sustainability to battle environmental impact.

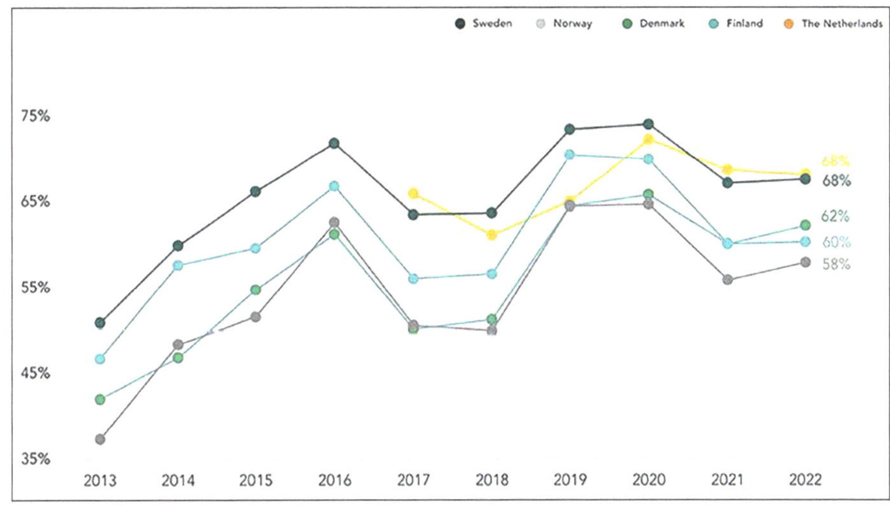

The consumers became aware of the impact of their actions in everyday life by buying the products for themselves and the environment. This propelled action leads to brand sustainability. The revamping of choosing sustainable product sales prevailed over non-sustainable products. Customers are keen on buying products that are eco-labelled, sustainable, and eco-friendly, and they put an embargo on companies that don't meet the standards.

The growth of green claims at national and international levels has increased, and sustainability has become an integral part of company agendas. However, the authentic information and enforcing the green claims are often vague and unclear greenwashing.

The European Commission (EU) states, 'Half of the green claims lack evidence'. The national enforcement authorities of the EU sweep examined hundreds of websites to analyse the false (green) claims in various garments, cosmetics and household equipment sectors. The significant alarming findings:

Over half of traders did not provide adequate data to support their green claim.

37% of cases incorporated environment-conscious, eco-friendly tags in their advertisements and statements, which are vague and unclear to mislead the consumer.

In 59% of cases, the proof is not readily available to back their green claim.

The recent Consumer Market Monitoring Survey relates 78% of customers' preferential choice to environmental impact when selecting household appliances.

(IV)   Improvement Measures

Adopting sustainable practices such as reducing energy consumption, altering green energy, using public transportation, and consuming locally sourced food can considerably reduce the environmental impact. Conserving water, reducing waste, and choosing eco-friendly products are easier ways to save the natural environment.

Restoring environmental reputations can be challenging, and brand images can be fragile and easily tainted by a single error. It takes years to rebuild the reputation and also to regain market capitalisation.

a) Strategies & Goals

- Abiding with Environmental legislation
- Creating a Green marketing concept
- Brand awareness of green positioning
- Environment, Social & Governance(ESG)

The companies are analysed by investors using Environment, Social & Governance (ESG) for ethical and sustainable practices. The research study by Deutsche Bank, conducted with 56 academic studies, exhibits that companies with higher ESG rating factors have lower debt and equity. The highly sustainable company portfolio has performed more than 34% return on assets and 16% on equity. There is a steady rise in socially responsible investment, and nearly $13 trillion is invested in companies with ESG standards.

- Incorporating company portfolio based on environment
- Technological advancement for innovation in R&D for alternate and new products.
- Concentrating on the Triple Bottom Line

The company's impact on 3 P's – Profit, People, and Planet. A successful business strategy focuses on financial fulfilment and ensuring one stays in business.

b) Execution Procedures

We can rethink and strategise operational functions on a smaller scale to reduce costs and maximise profits.

- Ethical sourcing, reducing energy consumption and restructuring logistics.
- Upgrade existing products into sustainable and eco-friendly ones.
- Refurbish company vehicles into eco-friendly models and energy-efficient ones.
- Incorporate carpool and bicycle sharing and encourage walking.
- Harnessing solar energy and utilising it for power consumption.
- Going digital and paperless office.
- Upgrading machinery for energy-efficient and utilisation
- Using eco-friendly products for packaging and marketing purposes.
- Contributing a part of the profit for supporting environmental causes – Joining 1% for the planet.

c) Recycling and Waste Management

Creating awareness and guidelines for workers about the environmental risks posed by chemicals or hazardous substances and waste disposal. Storing the waste and treating it before disposing it and ensuring it is collected by authorised licence waste collection and disposal. The company should treat the waste effluent before draining it into the allocated sewer system. The recycling materials should be separated and sent to appropriate recycling centres. If the business causes environmental damage such as noise, smoke, and fumes pollution, relevant steps must be taken to minimise damage control. According to regulations, appropriate bins should be used to ease waste recycling, and separating paper, glass, and metals will simplify waste management.

General wastage can be segregated and disposed of in the above-said manner. Still, according to a research study by Iowa University, hazardous substances need a whole new level of regulations to be adhered to. Dangerous substances like chemicals, toxic minerals, radioactive materials, electrical & electronics, and the list of 130 categories are considered substances that should not be dumped in landfills or sewer systems. When they come in contact with land, water or air, these substances threaten health and the environment.

Proper waste management, such as recycling, composting, and reusing materials, is essential for reducing the amount of landfill and minimising pollution. Recycling materials such as paper, plastic, glass, and metal helps to conserve natural resources and reduces the energy required to produce new products.

d) Conservation of Biodiversity and Natural Resources

We must preserve the loss of habitat, air, soil and water pollution and maintain the balance of living organisms. The intricate web of all living beings works harmoniously to support our survival, such as food, water and shelter. Being sensitive and responsible while utilising natural resources and building offices and factories near forests and protected biodiversity areas will reduce human interaction with other natural habitats.

When the balance of biodiversity is overwhelmingly threatened by the enormous growth of population and overconsumption, it is our primary duty to conserve the ecosystem. Introducing non-native and invasive species may distort the natural chronicle order, and we need to refrain from building factories and offices near ecologically sensitive and conservation areas.

How business can help biodiversity?

While many businesses are committed to securing biodiversity, many organisations are not entirely familiar with the consequences and are still considering and on the verge of implementing as the knowledge of the impacts of business on the environment is limited. Preserving biodiversity can also open doors to innovation and alternative methods, a new process that was not enforced earlier.

We may not voluntarily harm biodiversity, but our actions will create an inevitable domino effect on the environment. We all know 'Reduce,

Reuse, Recycle' terminology, but implementing it in our workforce requires a framework for reducing our resources, shortening energy demand to make the products, and reducing the amount of landfill and waste.

Protecting natural resources, such as forests, water bodies, and wildlife, is crucial for maintaining a natural, healthy environment. Supporting conservation efforts, advocating for sustainable land use practices, and preserving biodiversity are essential to protect the environment.

e) Human Impact I=PAT

The I=PAT (Ehrlich and Ehrlich 1981) equation reflects the human impact on the environment (I) as a function of total population size (P), affluence - Resources utilised (A), and Technology (T). Simply put, the human impact created on the environment when making the products is the outcome of the equation.

The Economics of Ecosystems & Biodiversity (TEEB), a global study report by G8, aimed to focus on and provide the necessary tools for businesses and enterprises to reduce costs and set forth business advantages.

The primary key points of the report emphasise:

- Analyse the Impacts and business reliability on Biodiversity and Ecosystem Services (BES)
- Minimise the repercussions of endangering BES and offsetting wherever it is required.
- Incorporate information, evaluate performances and structure the framework of BES guidelines.
- Synthesise BES into the core principles of Corporate Social Responsibility (CSR)

The distress over the impact of biodiversity loss by businesses has initiated the growth of consumers' global sales of organic food and drink. Increased health problems caused by pesticides and toxic air and water pollution catalyse the shift to organic and eco-friendly products. A supportive United Nations (UN) report comments that toxic pesticides in food produce claim 200,000 lives yearly. Organic product growth is expected to reach $380.84 billion in 2025 at a 14.5% compound annual growth rate (CAGR).

(V)   Energy Conservation

Reducing energy and changing to green energy is good for the environment and contributes much financial profit. A growing number of organisations are driving towards profits with purpose.

Many businesses are building more energy-efficient workplaces to reduce energy consumption and lower carbon footprint.

a) Green/Renewable Energy

A company with renewable energy can curb greenhouse gas emissions and help the environment. The energy choices of shifting to solar, wind, hydroelectric, geothermal and other clean energies are more feasible and profitable than building coal and power plants.

The Intergovernmental Panel on Climate Change (IPCC) by the United Nations Framework Convention on Climate Change (UNFCCC) special report reveals that global warming climatic change can be reduced by limiting it to 1.5 degrees and not higher to curb further damage to climate change.

The Production Gap Report 2023 by the UN Environment Programme limits the global warming increase by 1.5 °C to 2 °C.

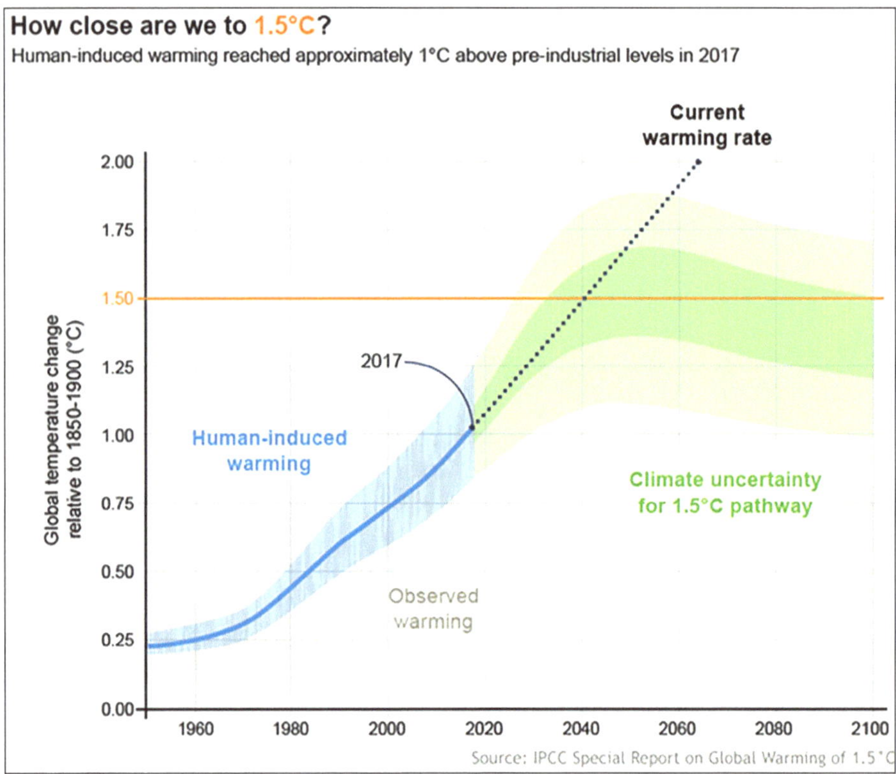

The current consequences of 1 degree by industrial and green gas emissions have destabilised weather conditions, rising sea levels and melting glaciers. Further increases in global warming will result in unprecedented and irreversible losses.

While the government and policymakers have progressive plans for net-zero emissions by 2050, it is up to the companies to adapt and shift to renewable energy to implement it.

- Sourcing green renewable energy sources. Reducing green gas emission reports will increase the company's social and credibility.
- Nominating contracts from energy providers with traceable renewable energy sources with Renewable Energy Guarantees of Origin (REGOs).

- Choosing a Corporate Power Purchasing Agreement (PPA) in agreement with energy supply from a specific clean green energy source.
- Sanctioning Production Tax Credit (PTC) to avail wind, solar, geothermal and other renewable sources.
- Allowance of Investment Tax Credit (ITC) for solar, thermal and wind turbine installation.

Corporate Clean Energy increased by 44% in 2019, three times higher than in 2017. Over 100 corporations have sanctioned 19.5GW of clean energy with a Power Purchasing Agreement (PPA). The technology sector is leading, followed by the oil and gas sectors.

When we discuss climatic change, the greenhouse gas released by fossil fuels is massive. Even though all countries have renewable energy policy targets, the tariffs, credits, costs, and available resources are the factors that inhibit the energy transformation.

b) Green Computing – Bring the Business to the Green Side

Green computing means consuming less energy to reduce the impact of technology on the environment. It reduces operational costs by 30% and is budget-friendly. Implementing green computing will steer the business forward while helping the environment.

- Choosing energy-efficient devices with a high energy star rating to reduce power consumption.
- Turning off and unplugging, hibernating, or using sleep mode on devices when not in use will considerably reduce power usage.
- Opting for cloud computing without any server maintenance is cost-effective. Maintaining a full-fledged IT department by going green is expensive for small and medium businesses.
- With the current COVID pandemic, the new normal of remote working and telecommuting results in less transport, reducing carbon footprint.

These sustainable activities will tremendously reduce carbon footprints and emissions, aiding social responsibility. This transformation benefits the company profile and helps society and the planet. Making minor necessary changes results in sustainable climatic change.

Environmental responsibility is a shared duty that requires combined effort to protect the planet for future generations. By understanding the issues and implementing effective remedies, we can overcome the adverse effects of human interference on the environment and promote sustainability. Individuals, communities, and governments must work together towards a greener and sustainable future. Promoting environmental awareness can ensure a healthier planet for future generations.

(VI) SDG – Targets & Indicators	
3 GOOD HEALTH AND WELL-BEING	
Target 3.9	By 2030, substantially reduce the number of deaths and illnesses from hazardous chemicals and air, water and soil pollution and contamination
Indicators 3.9.1	Mortality rate attributed to household and ambient air pollution
Indicators 3.9.2	Mortality rate attributed to unsafe water, unsafe sanitation and lack of hygiene (exposure to unsafe Water, Sanitation and Hygiene for All (WASH) services)
Indicators 3.9.3	Mortality rate attributed to unintentional poisoning

6 CLEAN WATER AND SANITATION	
Target 6.3	By 2030, improve water quality by reducing pollution, eliminating dumping and minimizing release of hazardous chemicals and materials, halving the proportion of untreated wastewater and substantially increasing recycling and safe reuse globally
Indicators 6.3.1	Proportion of domestic and industrial wastewater flows safely treated
Indicators 6.3.2	Proportion of bodies of water with good ambient water quality
7 AFFORDABLE AND CLEAN ENERGY	
Target 7.2	By 2030, increase substantially the share of renewable energy in the global energy mix
Target 7.3	By 2030, double the global rate of improvement in energy efficiency
Indicators 7.3.1	Energy intensity measured in terms of primal energy and GDP

8 DECENT WORK AND ECONOMIC GROWTH	
Target 8.4	Improve progressively through 2030, global resource efficiency in consumption and production and endeavor to decouple economic growth from environmental degradation, in accordance with the 10-year framework programmes on sustainable consumption and production, with developed countries taking the lead
Indicators 8.4.1	Material footprint, material footprint per capita, and material footprint per GDP
Indicators 8.4.2	Domestic material consumption, domestic material consumption per GDP
9 INDUSTRY, INNOVATION AND INFRASTRUCTURE	
Target 9.4	By 2030, upgrade infrastructure and retrofit industries to make them sustainable, with increased resource-use efficiency and greater adoption of clean and environmentally sound technologies and industrial processes, with all countries taking action in accordance with their respective capabilities
Indicators 9.4.1	CO_2 emission per unit of value added

11 SUSTAINABLE CITIES AND COMMUNITIES	
Target 11.4	Strengthen efforts to protect and safeguard the world's cultural and natural heritage
Indicators 11.4.1	Total per capita expenditure on the preservation, protection and conservation of all cultural and natural heritage, by source of funding (public, private), type of heritage (cultural, natural) and level of government (national, regional and local/municipal)
Target 11.6	By 2030, reduce the adverse per capita environmental impact of cities, including by paying attention to air quality and municipal and other waste management
Indicators 11.6.1	Proportion of urban solid waste regularly collected and with adequate final discharge out of total urban solid waste generated by the cities
Indicators 11.6.2	Annual mean levels of fine particulate matter (e.g. PM2.5 and PM10) in cities (population weighted)
12 RESPONSIBLE CONSUMPTION AND PRODUCTION	
Target 12.1	Implement the 10-year framework on programmes on sustainable consumption and production, all countries taking action, with developed countries taking the lead, taking into account the development and capabilities of developing countries

Indicators 12.1.1	Numbers of countries developing, adopting or implementing policy instruments aimed at supporting the shift to sustainable consumption and production
Target 12.4	By 2020, achieve the environmentally sound management of chemicals and all wastes throughout their cycle, in accordance with agreed international frameworks, and significantly reduce their release to air, water and soil in order to minimize their adverse impacts on human health and the environment
Indicators 12.4.1	Number of parties to international multilateral environmental agreements on hazardous waste, and other chemicals that meet their commitments and obligations in transmitting information as required by each relevant agreement
Indicators 12.4.2	(a) Hazardous waste generated per capita; and (b) proportion of hazardous waste treated, by type of treatment
Target 12.5	By 2030, substantially reduce waste generation through prevention, reduction, recycling and reuse
Indicators 12.5.1	National recycling rate, tons of material recycled
Target 12.6	Encourage companies, especially large and transnational companies, to adopt sustainable practices and to integrate sustainability information into their reporting cycle
Indicators 12.6.1	Number of companies publishing sustainability reports

15 LIFE ON LAND	
Target 15.2	By 2020, promote the implementation of sustainable management of all types of forests, halt deforestation, restore degraded forests and substantially increase afforestation and reforestation globally
Indicators 15.2.1	Progress towards sustainable forest management
Target 15.5	Take urgent and significant action to reduce the degradation of natural habitats, halt the loss of biodiversity and, by 2020, protect and prevent the extinction of threatened species
Indicators 15.5.1	Red List Index
Target 15.8	By 2020, introduce measures to prevent the introduction and significantly reduce the impact of the invasive alien species on land and water ecosystems and control or eradicate the priority species
Indicators 15.8.1	Proportion of countries adopting relevant national legislation and adequately resourcing the prevention or control of invasive alien species

Conclusion

Trade 4 Peace offers a convincing vision of a reality where participation and an ethical thriving economy suppress conflicts. By tackling the force of monetary trade, countries can comprehend and work towards a tranquil and amicable future. Consumers have now gained the awareness to make decisions based on social and ethical value trading more than ever. Companies must ensure that business practices are fair, sustainable, and socially responsible.

In summary, the fundamental shift in how businesses function with ethical practices not only gains reputation but also a strong loyalty customer base with financial benefits. We hold the power to influence and change the practices by our choices. We can foster a principled trading environment by supporting the brands and organisational practices that adhere to ethical trading practices.

In conclusion, the significance of trade in promoting peace cannot be overlooked. Through economic interdependence, cultural exchange, and conflict resolution mechanisms, trade is vital in fostering cooperation, stability, and understanding among nations. As we navigate an increasingly interconnected world, the transformative power of trade in building bridges and promoting peace remains essential for shaping a more harmonious future.

"We all know what the problems are, and we all know what we have promised to achieve. What is needed now is not more declarations or promises, but action to fulfil the promises already made." – Kofi Annan, Former Secretary-General, United Nations.

Trade 4 Peace Accreditation – Parameter Recommendations

1. ____

2. ____

3. ____

4. ____

5. ____

6. ____

7. ____

8. ____

9. ____

10. ____

We value your opinion, Please write your suggestions and upload it in the QR code.

10

Acknowledgements

My sincere appreciation goes to my friend Hemalatha, whose support and contribution were vital in shaping this book. She is accommodating with extensive research materials, extraordinary hours and matchless care when structuring the manuscript. Her insightful feedback has been a constant source of inspiration to strengthen the content.

Since the inception of this book, the directions have been tempered and enriched by economists from different countries with consistent suggestions. I thank everyone for their steadfast support, and this book could not have been completed without their unfailing and generous assistance.

Special Thanks To

A special thanks to Patrons of 'World Humanitarian Drive'

HE Anthony Thomas Aquinas Carmona SC, ORTT
5th President of Trinidad and Tobago

Erna Hennicot-Schoepges
First woman President of Luxembourg's Parliament

Fatmir Sejdiu
First President of Kosovo

Rt. Hon. Chris Philp M.P.
Shadow Leader of the House of Commons, U.K.

Reference list

Aaditya Mattoo, Stern, R.M. and Gianni Zanini (2008). *A handbook of international trade in services.* Oxford; New York: Oxford University Press.

Adams, F. (2010). *The United Nations in Latin America.* Routledge.

Arie Marcelo Kacowicz (2000). *Stable Peace Among Nations.* Rowman & Littlefield.

Breitenberg, M. (1993). *Directory of International and Regional Organisations Conducting Standards-Related Activities.* DIANE Publishing.

Buckley, R.P., Vai Io Lo and Boulle, L. (2008). *Challenges to multilateral trade: the impact of bilateral, preferential and regional agreements.* Alphen Aan Den Rijn: Kluwer Law International; Frederick, Md.

Captivating History (2020). *The Silk Road: A Captivating Guide to the Ancient Network of Trade Routes Established During the Han Dynasty of China and How It Conn.* Captivating History.

Chitadze, N. (2022). *Global dimensions of democracy and human rights: problems and perspectives.* Hershey PA: IGI Global, Information Science Reference (an imprint of IGI Global).

Cox, M., Ambika Flavel, Henson, I., Laver, J. and Wessling, R. (2014). *The scientific investigation of mass graves: towards protocols and standard operating procedures.* Cambridge: Cambridge University Press.

Crespo, N. and Simoes, N. (2021). *Handbook of Research on the Empirical Aspects of Strategic Trade Negotiations and Management.* IGI Global.

Daily, P. (2019). *Narrating China's Governance.* Springer Nature.

Davila, N. and Pina-Ramirez, W. (2018). *Effective Onboarding.* American Society for Training and Development.

Dunning, J.H., Mikoto Usui and International Economic Association. World Congress (1987). *Economic interdependence.* New York: St. Martin's Press.

Durlauf, S.N. and Blume, L.E. (2010). *Economic growth*. Basingstoke: Palgrave Macmillan.

Engelbrecht, M. (2015). *Asset Allocation in Private Banking*. BoD – Books on Demand.

Erik Oddvar Eriksen and John Erik Fossum (2015). *The European Union's Non-Members*. Routledge.

Esmaeili, H., Brand, V. and Karamanian, S.L. (2024). *International Trade with the Middle East and North Africa*. Taylor & Francis.

Fleisher, C.S. and Bensoussan, B.E. (2022). *Business and competitive analysis: effective application of new and classic methods*. Upper Saddle River, N.J.: Ft Press.

Fouad Sabry (2023). *Rule-Based System*. One Billion Knowledgeable.

Gipps, C.V. (1994). *Beyond testing: Towards a theory of educational assessment*. London; Washington: The Falmer Press.

Gitman, L.J., Mcdaniel, C. and Shah, A. (2023). *Introduction to Business*. Independently Published.

Grehan, J. (2013). *Churchill's Secret Invasion*. Pen and Sword.

Haar, B.M. (2008). *Front-End Vision and Multi-Scale Image Analysis*. Springer Science & Business Media.

Heritage, P. and Strozenberg, I. (2019). *The Art of Cultural Exchange*. Vernon Press.

Hoekman, B.M. and Mavroidis, P.C. (2015). *World Trade Organization (WTO)*. Routledge.

International Labour Office (2004). *Constitution of the International Labour Organization and standing orders of the International Labour Conference*. Geneva: Ilo.

Lim, C.L., Deborah Kay Elms and Low, P. (2012). *The Trans-Pacific Partnership: a quest for a twenty-first-century trade agreement*. Cambridge; New York: Cambridge University Press.

Lucie Qian Xia (2024). *The Diplomatic Making of EU-China Relations*. Taylor & Francis.

Mohamad Riad El Ghonemy (1998). *Affluence and poverty in the Middle East*. London; New York: Routledge.

Narang, N., Gartzke, E. and Kroenig, M. (2015). *Nonproliferation Policy and Nuclear Posture*. Routledge.

Nedumpara, J.J., Satwik Shekhar and Venkataraman, A. (2021). *Handbook on Product Standards and International Trade*. Kluwer Law International B.V.

Ng, E.S., Stamper, C.L., Alain Klarsfeld and Han, Y.J. (2021). *Handbook on Diversity and Inclusion Indices A Research Compendium*. Edward Elgar Publishing.

Papageorgiou, C. and Mr. Nicola Spatafora (2012). *Economic Diversification in LICs: Stylized Facts and Macroeconomic Implications*. INTERNATIONAL MONETARY FUND.

Prabhakaran Paleri (2022). *Revisiting National Security*. Springer Nature.

Preker, A.S., Zweifel, P., Schellekens, O.P. and World Bank (2010). *Global marketplace for private health insurance: strength in numbers*. Washington, D.C.: World Bank.

Ridgeway, C.L. (2011). *Framed by Gender*. Oxford University Press.

Robert Paul Weller (2019). *ALTERNATE CIVILITIES: democracy and culture in China and Taiwan*. S.L.: Routledge.

Sami Mahroum and Yasser Al-Saleh (2016). *Economic Diversification Policies in Natural Resource Rich Economies*. Routledge.

Schilling, M.A. (2023). *Strategic Management of Technological Innovation*. 7th ed. New York, Ny: Mcgraw-Hill Education.

Smith, P.J. (2013). *Global Trade Policy*. John Wiley & Sons.

Steger, D.P. (2010). *Redesigning the World Trade Organization for the Twenty-first Century*. Wilfrid Laurier Univ. Press.

Steinberg, R.M. (2011). *Governance, risk management, and compliance: it can't happen to us-avoiding corporate disaster while driving success*. Hoboken, N.J.: Wiley.

UNCTAD (2019). *Trade and Development Report 2018*. United Nations.

Xin, F. (2013). *Energy and Process Optimization for the Process Industries*. John Wiley & Sons.

Yannick Malevergne and Didier Sornette (2006). *Extreme Financial Risks*. Springer Science & Business Media.

Image Links

Global Gender Gap Report 2023 | World Economic Forum (weforum.org)

weforum.org/publications/global-gender-gap-report-2023/infographics-66115127a8/

https://www.unwomen.org/en/news/in-focus/csw61/equal-pay

https://www.who.int/publications/i/item/9789241564182

https://endchildlabour2021.org/5-takeaways-from-the-2021-global-estimates-on-child-labour/

https://www.weforum.org/agenda/2019/04/business-case-for-diversity-in-the-workplace/

https://www.weforum.org/agenda/2019/04/business-case-for-diversity-in-the-workplace/

https://www.weforum.org/agenda/2015/12/what-is-modern-slavery/#:~:text=People%20can%20be%20trafficked%20for,forced%20marriage%2C%20forced%20organ%20removal.

https://www.walkfree.org/global-slavery-index/map/#mode=data

https://www.unep.org/resources/emissions-gap-report-2023

https://sustonmagazine.com/2022/05/04/sustainable-brand-index-2022/

https://www.ipcc.ch/sr15/graphics/

Getting people with disabilities into work requires data | World Economic Forum (weforum.org)